Whitewater Valley Railroad: History Through the Miles

Barton Jennings

Whitewater Valley Railroad: History Through the Miles
Copyright © 2018 by Barton Jennings

All rights reserved. This book may not be duplicated or transmitted in any way, or stored in an information retrieval system, without the express written consent of the publisher, except in the form of brief excerpts or quotations for the purpose of review. Making copies of this book, or any portion, for any purpose other than your own, is a violation of United States copyright laws.

Publisher's Cataloging-in-Publication Data
Jennings, Barton

Whitewater Valley Railroad: History Through the Miles
120p.; 21cm.
ISBN: 978-1-7327888-0-0

Library of Congress Control Number: 2018912076

First Edition

Front cover photo by Barton Jennings
Back cover photo by Sarah Jennings

Please send comments or corrections to sarah@techscribes.com

TechScribes, Inc.
PO Box 620
Avon, IL 61415
www.techscribes.com

Printed in the United States of America

*for my friends at the
Whitewater Valley Railroad*

Other books by this author:

Arkansas & Missouri Railroad: History Through the Miles
Alaska Railroad: History Through the Miles
Iowa Interstate Railroad: History Through the Miles
Everett Railroad: History Through the Miles
Tennessee Central Railway: History Through the Miles

Contents

Preface 7
Whitewater River 9
White Water Valley Canal 13
    Construction 14
    Failure 15
    Preservation 17
Whitewater Valley Railroad 21
    White Water Valley Railroad 22
    Big Four Railroad 23
    Whitewater Valley Railroad 25
Whitewater Valley Railroad Equipment Roster 27
    Steam Locomotives 28
    Diesel Locomotives 32
    Passenger Cars 39
    Freight Cars 44
    Cabooses 49
Route Guide of the Whitewater Valley Railroad 55
About the Author 119

WWV 25 curves onto the Whitewater River bridge near Laurel with a special photographers charter train. Photo by Barton Jennings.

Dearborn Tower is featured in this night photo. Photo by Barton Jennings.

Photo by Barton Jennings.

Preface

The Indiana route used by the Whitewater Valley Railroad has a long transportation history. It started as the Whitewater River, then became the White Water Valley Canal, built along the Whitewater River around 1840. By 1865, the canal was dead and the railroad took over. Once operated by New York Central's "Big Four" – Cleveland, Cincinnati, Chicago & St. Louis Railway – today the line between Connersville and Metamora is operated by the Whitewater Valley Railroad, a tourist railroad providing service to the former canal town of Metamora.

Today's Whitewater Valley Railroad is a not-for-profit corporation, created in 1972 and operating their first passenger trains in 1974. The original operations used 25 miles of leased track between Connersville and Brookville, owned by Penn Central. After flooding washed out the railroad between Metamora and Brookville, Penn Central obtained trackage rights to Connersville and abandoned their own route along the Whitewater River. The Whitewater Valley Railroad was able to lease, and later buy, the line north of Metamora, today's route of the Valley Flyer passenger train.

Today, passengers can ride a route that dates from the 1860s and looks similar to what it has for more than 150 years. The track has been rebuilt, the passenger cars date from the 1920s and 1930s, and examples of some of the first diesel locomotives pull the train. Volunteers operate the railroad, and many will point out historic sites along the route. However, this book is written for those who want to know more about the route of the railroad, often answering the question of, "Where are we and what once happened here?"

Whitewater River

The Whitewater River is actually two rivers, both forming in Indiana. The East Fork Whitewater River forms near New Madison, Indiana, while the West Fork Whitewater River forms southeast of Muncie, Indiana. The East Fork is slightly less than 60 miles long and flows south to Brookville where it joins the West Fork. About two miles north of Brookville is Brookville Lake, built 1968-74 by the U.S. Army Corps of Engineers. The purpose of the 17-mile-long lake is to control flooding problems around Brookville, and on the Ohio River.

The West Fork, considered by some sources to be the primary channel, is approximately 60 miles long and is located about a dozen miles west of the East Fork. The two branches follow each other closely for their entire length before merging near Brookville. Once merged, the Whitewater River flows to the southeast about 30 miles before flowing into the Miami River, a tributary of the Ohio River.

The Whitewater River is a rural river, with agriculture being the primary land use within the watershed. Because of this, species diversity in the West Fork Whitewater River and Whitewater River is reported by conservation studies to be above average compared to other major streams in Indiana. The watershed of the river is generally steep, and the river has a steep drop for this part of the country. Several sources state that the Whitewater River is the swiftest river in Indiana because it falls an average of six feet per mile. It passes through thick deposits of sand and gravel left behind by retreating glaciers, forming small rapids and attracting some early stone industries.

The Whitewater River was an early route for settlers moving into the Indiana area. In the late 1700s, the area was the home of the Miami Indians, with the Potawatomi and Shawnee also in the region. The area had also recently become the home of the Delaware Indians, moved here from the east. The first written record was by Jacob Parkhurst, who hunted the southern part of the Whitewater River Valley in the winter of 1790-91. Others visited the valley over the next few years, but it wasn't until the local Indians were defeated by General "Mad" Anthony Wayne in 1794 at the Battle of Fallen Timbers that the territory became safe for white settlement. Fallen Timbers was the final battle of the Northwest Indian War, a war where British troops supported a number of tribes against the new United States. The result was the Treaty of Greenville, signed on August 3, 1795, that ceded Indian land to the United States government and reaffirmed that the Northwest Territory was part of the United States.

The Territory Northwest of the Ohio River (Northwest Territory) was claimed by various states, including Connecticut, Massachusetts, New York, and Virginia. However, the Territory was set aside as a separate governmental territory, and later became the states of Ohio, Indiana, Illinois, Michigan, Wisconsin, and part of Minnesota. On May 7, 1800, the United States divided the Northwest Territory into two areas and named the western section the Indiana Territory so that the eastern part could become the new State of Ohio. During this time, the Whitewater River provided a route from the well-traveled Ohio River into the region.

During the spring of 1801, three Moravian missionaries traveled the river and found that settlers were already starting farms in the area. Their report indicated that most of the settlers had crossed the Ohio River from Kentucky and that they were often trading with the few Indians left in the Territory, many camped near today's Brookville. Local governments began to be organized, and the first records of land ownership were recorded in May, 1803. Over the next few years, entire families and communities moved to the area, including those from Pennsylvania, South and North Carolina, Virginia, New Jersey and Maryland. On December 11, 1816, Indiana became the 19th state, using a name that means "Indian Name" or "Land of the Indians." Today, it is the 38th largest state by area and the 17th most populated. Indianapolis is the capital and largest city in the state. However, while the Whitewater River Valley is still mostly a rural region of the state, this is where much of the state's development began.

Because the river varied between floods and droughts, and the channel was not always reliable for small boats, the idea of a canal soon swelled among the local farmers and communities. Efforts were made in the 1820s to fund and build a canal, but it wasn't until the 1830s that construction actually began. The history of the canal and the railroad that replaced it follows. However, with the canal service gone and the railroad now a route for tourism, the Whitewater River has returned to many of its earlier characteristics. It still drains much of central and southeastern Indiana, with the river levels varying based upon the rain and snow across the region. The river today is popular for recreation, with the East Fork the source of Brookville Lake, and a part of Whitewater State Park and the Martindale State Fishing Area. The West Fork Whitewater River is popular for fishing and canoeing, although there are no official Indiana river access points.

Gordon's Lock # 24 (or Millville Lock) is an example of what a working lock on the White Water Valley Canal would have looked like. Photo by Sarah Jennings.

White Water Valley Canal

During the late 1700s and early 1800s, the primary manmade transportation systems were roads and canals. Roads were quick and relatively cheap to build, but they had great limitations in the amount of freight that could be moved. However, canals allow hundreds and even thousands of tons of freight to be moved on a single vessel. For many towns, the canal was the answer for their economic prosperity.

The towns along the Whitewater River saw an opportunity to connect their industries and farms with the rest of the country by building a canal alongside the existing stream. The first efforts to build the canal took place in 1822-23 when a convention of delegates from area counties met in Hamilton, Ohio, to plan for such a project. The convention resulted in a survey of possible routes by Colonel Shriver's Brigade of the United States Engineers. Winter weather stopped the project and it wasn't until 1834 that further work took place. A plan for the canal was released in 1835 with an estimated cost per mile of $14,908, or $1,142,126 for the entire canal.

On January 27, 1836, Indiana Governor Noah Noble signed "An Act to Provide for a General System of Internal Improvements" to create a board to fund and oversee the construction of a number of canals, roadways, and railroads throughout the state. These improvements included the Wabash and Erie Canal, the Madison & Indianapolis Railroad, the Indiana Central Canal, and the Whitewater Canal. The Whitewater Canal (also spelled White Water Canal in some documents) was intended to extend from Lawrenceburg, on the Ohio River near Cincinnati, northward to Hagerstown, and was to receive $1.4 million in state funding. A second canal was chartered in Ohio to extend the canal from Harrison, Ohio, to Cincinnati. The route was quickly surveyed and designed, and contracts for building the canal were let at Brookville, Indiana, on September 13, 1836.

Construction

Construction on the canal proceeded quickly, and the canal opened from Lawrenceburg to Brookville in 1839 at a reported cost of $664,665. The *Ben Franklin* became the first canal boat to reach Brookville, arriving on June 8, 1839, to great celebration. At the time, much of the work was also completed to Cambridge City. However, in the same year, the State of Indiana, which was paying for the construction of the canal, found itself heavily in debt, owing more than $14 million. All public works programs were abandoned, leaving the future of the canal uncertain. The solution was the chartering of the White Water Valley Canal Company by the 1841-1842 state legislature, giving the new company the right to operate and extend the canal.

The new company's promotion was headed by Samuel W. Parker of Connersville, and his success likely led to his later election to Congress. Thomas Tyner, who was one of the principal contractors of the initial construction, was hired to restart the construction. Parker was chosen to dig the first wheelbarrow of dirt, an event marked by celebrations along the route, and a major thunderstorm that quickly ended the event. By October 1843, the line had been extended up the Whitewater River to Laurel, and east to Cincinnati via the Cincinnati and Whitewater Canal. Connersville was reached in June 1845 and Cambridge City in October 1845. The *Patriot* became the first canal boat to arrive at Connersville in the Fall of 1845. By this time, the company had spent $473,000 on the project and had not yet reached its ultimate goal.

Construction was halted on January 1, 1847 when a series of storms flooded and damaged the canal. Several aqueducts were destroyed, feeder dams and canals were damaged, and some locks were taken out of service. Almost $100,000 was spent to repair the damage, and the canal opened to Hagerstown late that year by the Hagerstown Canal Company. By this time, the canal's total length was 76 miles, not including a 25-mile spur on into Cincinnati built by the State of Ohio. The canal used 56 locks to climb approximately 500 feet out of the Ohio River valley, a steep climb for such a short canal. In addition to the locks, there were 7 dams, aqueducts over 10 creeks, and 2 more across the West Fork of the

Whitewater River. At several points hills forced the canal into the river, which required work to enlarge and maintain the channel.

A second flood caused almost $80,000 damage in November 1848. It was slowly repaired, but the construction of railroads across the region ended most boat service. An 1858 lawsuit by several contractors and bond holders who had not been fully paid led to the courts appointing a receiver to try and save the company. The case was so complicated and controversial that it went all the way to the U.S. Supreme Court. The receiver was appointed with the responsibility of trying to run the canal and pay off the debt.

This historical marker stands near the shops of the railroad at Connersville. Photo by Sarah Jennings.

Failure

Users of the canal, both shippers and carriers, continued to fight to save the route. Several lawsuits attempted to prevent abandonment of the canal while others organized to buy it. However, the canal only served boats from 1839 until 1865. The *Indiana American* newspaper in Brookville had a large article about efforts to save the canal in their April 24, 1865, issue. Happening just a month before the end of the Civil War, the newspaper reported that mill owners and others had proposed to acquire the canal to preserve water power and to restore navigation between Brookville and Connersville. The newspaper excitedly editorialized "Subscription papers are now in circulation....and it is hoped our farmers and business men generally will donate liberally, as it is of the utmost importance that our mills be again put in operation, and transportation of some kind afforded us. It is useless to await the action of the Canal Company, as the Receiver has declined to render any assistance whatever."

In December 1865, the Connersville Hydraulic Company was organized to acquire parts of the canal waterway and to use its water flow for hydraulic uses, supporting the many mills along its route. The receiver and the United States Circuit Court of the Southern District of Indiana authorized a lease of the canal in February 1866. A report from the time stated that the Hydraulic Company controlled the canal and related feeder facilities from Cambridge City to Heron's Lock, located about one mile below Connersville. The company was managed by several members of the Roots family, including Philander Higley Roots, Francis Marion Roots, D. T. Roots, and F. T. Roots. They represented the management and owners of the P. H. and F. M. Roots Company, later the Roots Blower Company. The hydraulic firm was generally successful, and the canal was maintained for this use until 1936. There were actually proposals as late as the 1950s to maintain the canal for this purpose.

The end of the canal also came from the railroads. The Indianapolis & Cincinnati Railroad Company bought the Cincinnati branch of the canal in 1862 with plans to replace it with a railroad. While Indiana residents protested the sale, there was little that they could do to stop the actions of the State of Ohio. However, efforts to replace the canal with a railroad in Indiana could be slowed. An 1863 auction sale of the White Water Valley Canal to Henry C. Lord, president of the Indianapolis & Cincinnati Railroad, for $65,000 was halted due to state law. However, a change in the law allowed the canal to be sold in 1865 for the same purpose.

Preservation

The history of the canal did not end with the railroads or the conversion to a hydraulic canal. Even the final abandonment of the canal didn't end its existence. On October 24, 1941, a number of area residents created the Whitewater Canal Association to acquire the remains of the canal from the Laurel Feeder Dam to Brookville. This was a part of the canal that was not destroyed by the railroad, and in fact had been used by the Brookville & Metamora Hydraulic Company until the 1920s. The Whitewater Canal Association was incorporated in 1942 and acquired almost 15 miles of the canal, negotiated for easements where necessary, and began some minor repairs. The organization also campaigned for the State of Indiana to preserve the former White Water Valley Canal. This came about on February 27, 1945, when the state authorized the Indiana Conservation Commission to take over the canal controlled by the Whitewater Canal Association and to begin maintaining it. Since then, parts of the canal have been stabilized while others have been watered again with operating canals.

The section preserved includes the canal town of Metamora, along with its operating grist mill, canal locks, and possibly the last existing covered wooden aqueduct in the United States. Much of this area is now part of the Whitewater Canal State Historic Site, with parts listed on various historical lists such as the National Civil Engineering Landmark Program and the National Register of Historic Places. There is an operating canal boat – the *Ben Franklin III* – that provides a 25-minute cruise on the canal, tours of the Metamora Grist Mill, and lots of opportunity to explore the Metamora area.

Besides the remains of the canal and locks, there is one more very impressive survivor of the White Water Valley Canal, the former headquarters at 111 East Fourth Street in Connersville. The building was built in 1842 and was known as The Canal House. It is an impressive two-story, Greek Revival style stone building which certainly looks like a temple. Initially, the canal company was so busy that they had their own bank in the building. They also printed their own currency here, a common practice by banks of the era. After the canal closed, the building housed a bank (Savings Bank of Indiana from 1854 until 1857), and then became the residence of Dr. S. W. Vance and family (1857-1936), and then Congressman Finly Hutchinson Gray and his wife from 1936 to 1947. Next, it was the home of the local chapter of the Veterans of Foreign Wars (1947-1971). The organization Historic Connersville now owns the building and uses it for multiple events. The building was added to the National Register of Historic Places in 1973.

The Canal House is a solid reminder of the canal era of Connersville. Photo by Sarah Jennings.

Another preservation and educational effort is the Whitewater Canal Scenic Byway. The Byway has been described by several groups as telling "a story of the past and growth during an early developmental period of the United States and Indiana." It includes Indiana Highway 121 which follows the canal, railroad and river.

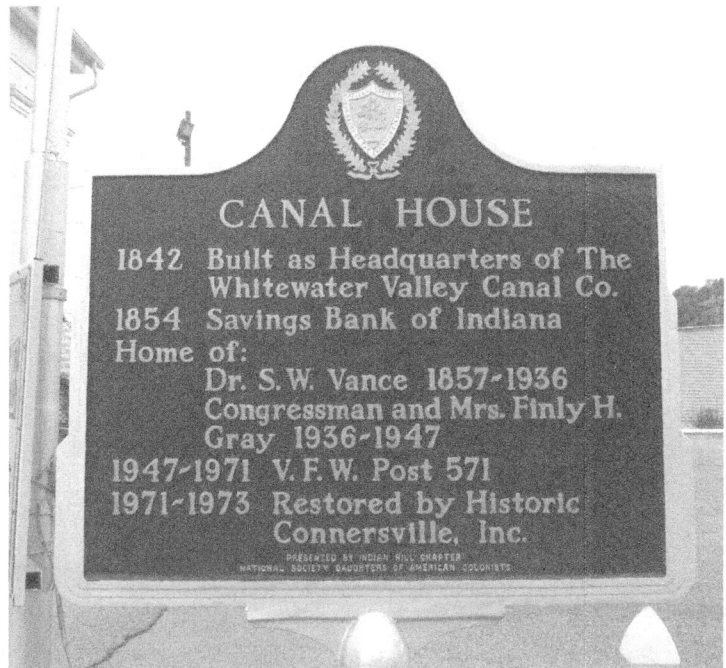

This historical marker stands next to the Canal House in Connersville. Photo by Sarah Jennings.

Photo by Sarah Jennings.

Whitewater Valley Railroad

The Whitewater Canal was the first Indiana canal to be replaced by a railroad. After a series of financial failures and storms whose damage could not be fully repaired, the White Water Valley Canal Company was in the hands of a receiver, appointed in 1855. By the early 1860s, even more bills were unpaid and routine maintenance on the canal was not being performed. Soon, locks didn't work and water levels were insufficient for canal boats. This led to an 1863 public auction in Brookville. At the auction, a United States marshal sold the Indiana part of the White Water Valley Canal to Henry C. Lord, president of the Indianapolis & Cincinnati Railroad. A price of $65,000 was offered, but the sale was halted due to questions about whether Indiana law would allow a canal partly funded by the State of Indiana to be sold and replaced by a railroad.

While the canal was popular, a petition drive began to get the legislature to pass a law that would allow such a sale. Reportedly more than one thousand residents signed the petition and the Indiana government soon enacted new laws that would allow such a sale, primarily an "Act to authorize Railroad Companies to occupy and use for railroad purposes the property of Canal Companies, with their consent." The law was approved in November 1865 and included a provision that would allow parts of the canal to be used for hydraulic purposes, as desired by the Connersville Hydraulic Company.

In early December 1865, parts of the canal were leased to the Connersville Hydraulic Company, with the Brookville & Metamora Hydraulic Company leasing the Laurel to Brookville section. At the same time, C. C. Binkley, president of the White Water Valley Canal Company, again sold the canal route to Henry C. Lord. The delay had benefitted the canal company as the new sale price was $137,348.12. With these leases and sale, the canal as a transportation mode had ended.

By the early 1850s, canals were already being replaced by railroads as they were cheaper to build, were faster, operated in both winter and summer, and generally had greater freight and passenger capacities. The construction of new canals was slowing and railroads were building all across the country. In 1840, there were almost three thousand miles of railroad track in the United States, nine thousand miles by 1850, and more than thirty thousand miles by 1860. Even during the Civil War, new railroads were being built throughout the north and west. Therefore, the story of the White Water Valley Canal becoming the White Water Valley Railroad is not uncommon.

White Water Valley Railroad

When Henry C. Lord, president of the Indianapolis & Cincinnati Railroad, bought the canal, the property was assigned to the White Water Valley Railroad, incorporated on June 8, 1865. Construction on the railroad had already begun on the Ohio canal as that part of the sale was allowed. West of Valley Junction, construction continued and the railroad reached Connersville in the spring of 1867, and Hagerstown, Indiana, in 1868 (18 miles built in 1865, 36 in 1866, and 8 in 1867). This created a through railroad from Cincinnati to Hagerstown, with a connection on to Chicago, that attracted larger railroads. The Indianapolis, Cincinnati & Lafayette Railway (created in 1867 from several lines, including the first railroad built in Indiana, as a Cincinnati to Indianapolis system) operated the line until May 1, 1871. For several years after that date, the White Water Valley Railroad ran its own trains.

The *Ninth Annual Report of the Commissioner of Railroads and Telegraphs of Ohio for the Year Ending June 30, 1875*, provided some information about the railroad at the time. It stated that the White Water Valley Railroad operated from North Bend, Ohio, to Hagerstown, Indiana, 72 miles of single track mainline, and 6.851 miles of sidings and other tracks. The report stated that the White Water Valley Railroad operated the Harrison Branch Railroad and the Cincinnati & Whitewater Valley Railroad, both in Ohio. These two railroads combined for about nine miles of track into the Cincinnati area. However, not all information was available at the time "owing to the line and effects of the lessee being placed in hands of a receiver."

Whitewater Valley Railroad

The Harrison Branch Railroad started as a partnership created on August 17, 1864, to replace the White Water Valley Canal with a railroad. With the legal issues in Indiana, only the canal in Ohio was initially converted to a railroad. This created a railroad from Valley Junction, Ohio, to the Indiana-Ohio border at Harrison. The Harrison Branch Railroad Company was incorporated on December 6, 1871, to take over the railroad, and it was almost immediately leased by the White Water Valley Railroad.

The Cincinnati & White Water Valley Railroad Company was incorporated on June 28, 1873, to build about two miles of track between Valley Junction and the Ohio River at North Bend. The purpose of the new railroad was to bypass a tunnel on the original line built by the Cincinnati & Indiana Railroad. The Ohio report stated that the railroad "was built in the interest of the White Water Valley Railroad Company of Indiana, by whom it is leased."

The 62-mile long railroad was sold at a foreclosure sale on May 15, 1878, to a reorganization committee. An advertisement in the December 12, 1878, issue of *The Railway Age* promoted the "Sale of Railroad Equipment" of the Whitewater Valley Railroad. The equipment listed as being for sale included "locomotives Nos. 1, 2, 3 and 6, two passenger cars, one baggage and mail car, seventy box cars, thirty flat cars, thirty coal cars, thirty stock cars, two cabooses, and one complete set of air brakes." On May 28, 1878, the White Water Railroad Company was incorporated to operate the line, and assumed ownership on May 12, 1879.

Big Four Railroad

Local control of the railroad had some benefits, but the reliance on connections at either end of the railroad kept it a small rural operation. However, the line could potentially play a role as part of a through line, and on November 1, 1890, the Cleveland, Cincinnati, Chicago & St. Louis Railway Company (CCC&StL) obtained control of the White Water Railroad. The larger railroad, known as the Big Four for the cities in its name, almost immediately made use of the line. Commuter trains operated between Connersville and Cincinnati, explaining the turntable at Connersville. Through trains and parlor cars were also operated from Cincinnati to Fort Wayne, changing at Connersville to the tracks of the Lake Erie & Western. This practice of using the Lake Erie & Western, later the Nickel Plate Road and Norfolk & Western, became common for all trains as the line north of Beesons to Hagerstown was abandoned in 1931. The White Water Railroad was fully acquired by the Big Four on June 16, 1915.

The Big Four was acquired by the New York Central in 1906, but the smaller railroad was allowed to operate as a separate company until 1930. During the Depression of the 1930s, the New York Central assumed additional control of the CCC&StL, even though employee timetables continued to state "Cleveland, Cincinnati, Chicago & St. Louis Railway – The N.Y.C.R.R.Co. Leasee." Under the New York Central, the line continued the trend of fewer trains. While daily passenger service over this line peaked at about a dozen daily trains during World War I, service dropped almost immediately after the war. During the late 1920s and early 1930s, the New York Central used a doodlebug motorcar on its daily Connersville to Cincinnati roundtrip, making 22 stops each way on the run. All passenger service on the line ended in 1933. Stations were also closed and the agency hours were cut back, so that by 1951, only Laurel and Connersville had a weekday agent, and Alpine, Nulltown, and Metamora were listed as having no facilities.

The last steam locomotive operated on the Whitewater route in March 1957, just months before the last steam locomotive on the entire New York Central operated in the Cincinnati area on May 2, 1957. On February 1, 1968, the New York Central merged with the Pennsylvania Railroad to form the Penn Central Transportation Company. Almost immediately, Penn Central was in financial troubles and service was cut across the system. Freight service was discontinued south of Connersville in 1972. However, Penn Central continued to provide switch service between Connersville and Beesons to serve the large Philco-Ford plant. When Penn Central became part of Conrail in 1976, Philco-Ford was switched by Conrail. In 1981, this small isolated section was sold to the Indiana Hi-Rail, and has since gone through several other operators.

Whitewater Valley Railroad

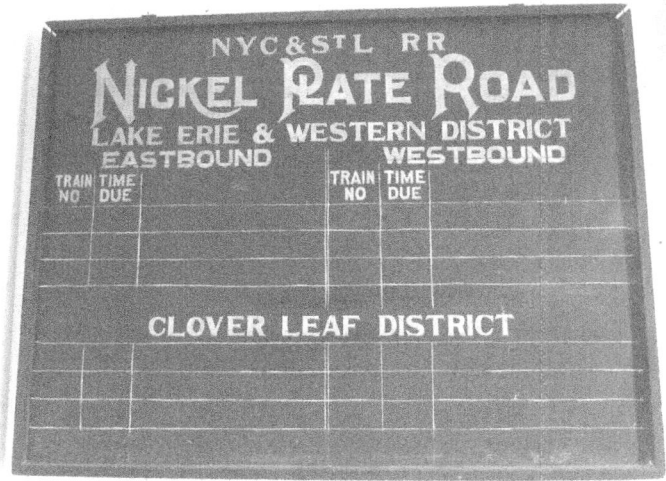

This former Nickel Plate Road train schedule board can today be found in the Connersville station of the Whitewater Valley Railroad. Photo by Sarah Jennings.

Whitewater Valley Railroad

In 1974, the non-profit Whitewater Valley Railroad leased the line between Connersville and Brookville from Penn Central for excursion purposes. Since then, tourist railroad service has been conducted over nineteen miles of track between Connersville and Metamora. The railroad actually ran on to Brookville the first year but cut the route back to Metamora before the 1975 season due to a track washout and Penn Central's application to abandon the line between Brookville and Metamora. The 26-mile line east of Brookville was sold to the Indiana & Ohio Railroad in 1979. The Whitewater Valley Railroad bought 18 miles of track in 1983 and then bought the northernmost mile from the Indiana Hi-Rail Corporation. The Whitewater Valley line is all 90# rail, some laid as early as 1897. This indicates the slow progression from Cincinnati-Indianapolis mainline to rural branchline that the railroad experienced.

The operations of the Whitewater Valley Railroad are conducted by volunteers, who also maintain and restore the track, locomotives, passenger cars, and freight cars owned by the organization. Little of the equipment was acquired in useable condition, and large investments are required annually to keep the track and trains together. Funding comes from ticket and souvenir sales, donations, and special events.

Today, the Whitewater Valley Railroad operates their *Valley Flyer* from Connersville to Metamora most weekends from early May until late October. In addition, the railroad operates the *Metamora Local*, a short train ride to the end of the line southeast of town. A number of other special event trains also operate over parts of the railroad, providing many opportunities to experience the one-time route of the White Water Valley Canal.

NYC 9339 poses at the Dearborn Tower. Photo by Barton Jennings.

Whitewater Valley Railroad Equipment Roster

The Whitewater Valley Railroad operates passenger excursion trains using historic diesel locomotives and coaches from several different railroads. The passenger cars once carried passengers on railroads such as Erie, New York Central, and Rock Island. In addition to these locomotives and passenger cars, the non-profit organization owns a large number of other pieces of railroad equipment, including steam and diesel locomotives, passenger and freight cars, cabooses, and track equipment. While many have been restored, others are waiting their turn through the restoration shop.

The list of equipment below is accurate at the time of the writing of this book. However, additional equipment can always be obtained, swapped between museums, or even used to restore other cars. The history for some equipment can be difficult to determine, but it is provided when known.

WWV 25 at Leonards (Lennards). Photo by Barton Jennings.

Steam Locomotives

No steam locomotives are currently in regular service on the Whitewater Valley Railroad. However, several visiting steamers have recently operated on the line and there have been restoration efforts on one or more of the steam locomotives owned by the railroad.

No.	Original Owner	Builder and History
3	unknown	This small 2-truck Heisler locomotive was built in 1906 and went through several owners before being sold to South Carolina's Santee River Hardwood Company as their #3. In 1962, it was sold to the Maggie Valley Amusement Corporation and became Highlander Railroad #3, and then Maggie Valley Railroad #3. It was sold to the Whitewater Valley Railroad in 1974 and operated for several years. Reportedly it has been sold but is still stored on the railroad.

Equipment Roster

6	East Broad Top Railroad	This 0-6-0 locomotive was built by Baldwin Locomotive Works in February 1907 with Builder's Number 30046. It was one of several standard gauge steam engines built for the interchange work of the East Broad Top Railroad and Coal Company. This was actually the third #6 engine. #6 is noted as having been sealed up in the Mount Union (PA) enginehouse when the railroad closed. It was sold to the Whitewater Valley Railroad in 1975. It operated here for several years and is currently awaiting a complete restoration. There has been some discussion about selling #6 to a Pennsylvania museum to return it home.
11	Southwestern Portland Cement	This 0-4-0T industry locomotive was built by Vulcan Iron Works in December 1924 with Builder's Number 3492. When retired, #11 was placed on display at the company's office at Fairborn, Ohio, in 1957. It came to the Whitewater Valley in late 1992.

6894	New York Central Railroad	Locomotives of this type routinely worked at Connersville. This 0-6-0 locomotive was built by the Pittsburgh Works of the American Locomotive Company in June 1912 with Builder's Number 51245. Originally #8794, it was a class B-10W switch engine assigned to the Michigan Central subsidiary. It became #6894 in 1936. In November 1945, #6894 became Wyandotte Southern Railroad #7, then Nicholson Terminal and Dock Company #15 in June, 1950. Following retirement, #6894 went through the hands of several rail enthusiasts and a scrapper, being stored in Hagerstown, Maryland. It was eventually donated by Mr. Charles Smith and the estate of H. Lansing Vail to the Whitewater Valley Railroad in 2005. It is the only surviving B-10 switcher of 683 B-10 and B-11 engines bought by the NYC.

Equipment Roster

WWV 11 0-4-0T, Connersville. Photo by Barton Jennings.

Diesel Locomotives

The Whitewater Valley Railroad is very unique in that it possesses diesel locomotives from six major builders. This includes American Locomotive Company (Alco), Baldwin Locomotive Works, Electro-Motive, General Electric, Lima Locomotive Works, and Plymouth Locomotive Works. Most are smaller switcher-type locomotives used in yards or for local service, very representative of the power once used on this route.

No.	Original Owner	Builder and History
1	U.S. Navy	This is a 65-ton centercab General Electric locomotive. During World War II, both the U.S. Navy and Army acquired a large number of these small diesel locomotives to switch ammunition depots. As they were retired, they were auctioned off or made available to non-profit organizations. This locomotive is lettered as U.S. Navy 1, Navy Yard Puget Sound, USN 65-00053. The final number was for the entire navy locomotive roster.
8	Muncie & Western Railroad	General Electric built this 70-tonner in December 1946, with Builder's Number 28505, for the subsidiary of the Ball Brothers Company glass jar manufacturing firm in Muncie, Indiana. The Whitewater Valley Railroad acquired the locomotive in 1995.

25	Cincinnati Union Terminal	Lima Locomotive Works built this LS-750 switcher in June, 1951, with Builder's Number 9541. It is the only existing LS-750 locomotive of six built. The designation LS-750 was never made official by Lima, but instead is generally used to describe a Lima 750 horsepower switch engine. The locomotive later went to the Cadillac & Lake City tourist railroad. It was the first locomotive owned by the Whitewater Valley Railroad.
99	Patapsco & Back Rivers	This diesel locomotive was built by Baldwin Locomotive Works as unit DF100 for dual fuel testing in December 1949 with Builder's Number 74640. It was sold to the Patapsco & Back Rivers Railroad as #335 in 1953. It later went to Charleston, West Virginia, and became Amherst Industries #99, then Whitewater Valley Railroad #99 in 2001. The locomotive was originally designed as a model DS-4-4-1000, then S-12.
210	Calumet & Hecla Mining	General Electric built this 70-tonner in December 1946 using Builder's Number 28566. It was sold to the Marquette & Huron Mountain Railroad in May 1972. Cargill later used the locomotive.

320	Baltimore & Ohio	Lima Locomotive Works built this LS-1200 switcher in December, 1950, with Builder's Number 9468. The designation LS-1200 was never made official by Lima, but instead is generally used to describe a Lima 1200 horsepower switch engine. Only 69 of this model were ever manufactured. In 1965, the locomotive was sold to the American Rolling Mill Company (ARMCO) as their #E-123 at Middletown, Ohio. It came to the Whitewater Valley in 1987.
346	Patapsco & Back Rivers	This diesel locomotive was built by Baldwin Locomotive Works as Patapsco & Back Rivers Railroad #346 in September 1951, with Builder's Number 75235. It later became Amherst Industries #100 in Charleston (WV), then Whitewater Valley Railroad #346. The locomotive was designed as a model S-12. It came to the Whitewater Valley Railroad with #99 in 2001.
532	Milwaukee Road	This locomotive was built by EMD (the Electro-Motive Division of General Motors) as an SD9 in January 1954. It carried Builder's Number 18771 and Chicago, Milwaukee, St. Paul & Pacific Railroad #2226. It was rebuilt in October 1975 to what was known as an SD-10, becoming #532. The locomotive later became Soo Line #532 before being donated to the Whitewater Valley Railroad by Canadian Pacific in 2001.

709	Armco Steel Corporation	Lima Locomotive Works built this LS-1000 switcher in March, 1950, with Builder's Number 9400. The designation LS-1000 was never made official by Lima, but instead is generally used to describe a Lima 1000 horsepower switch engine. Only 38 of this model were ever manufactured.
2561	Wagner Quarries	This is a Plymouth Locomotive Works ML-6 gasoline locomotive, built in January 1930. The locomotive is listed as a 30-ton unit, powered by a six-cylinder engine and uses a four-speed manual clutch transmission. It has Builder's Number 3382. It was built for the Sandusky quarry of Wagner Quarries, and then it went to the France Stone Company #2 at Monroe, Michigan.
9339	Proctor and Gamble	This Alco is a model S-1, built as Proctor and Gamble #9 in January 1948 with Builder's Number 75534. It came to the Whitewater Valley Railroad in 1986 and has been painted as a New York Central locomotive.

Locomotive 25 was the first diesel owned by the railroad. Photo by Barton Jennings.

WWV 99, Connersville. Photo by Barton Jennings.

Equipment Roster

The WWV has returned this Baldwin to its original Patapsco & Black Rivers RR 346 in this photo at Connersville. Photo by Barton Jennings.

WWV 210 GE 70-ton, Connersville. Photo by Barton Jennings.

Whitewater Valley Railroad: History Through the Miles

WWV 709, Connersville. Photo by Barton Jennings.

NYC 9339 switches at Connersville. Photo by Barton Jennings.

Passenger Cars

The passenger car fleet used by the Whitewater Valley Railroad primarily consists of coaches used in local or commuter service. Most were built in the 1920s and 1930s and feature open windows. They come from such railroads as Erie, New York Central, and the Chicago, Rock Island & Pacific. Many of the cars have the Whitewater Valley Railroad's number near the doorway, with the original owner and number at the middle of the car.

No.	Original Owner	Builder and History
1	Erie Railroad	This coach was built as Erie #2471 by Pullman in 1934. It is known as a Stillwell car for its designer L.B. Stillwell. Stillwell had earlier worked for Westinghouse Electric and Manufacturing Company, and was heavily involved with creating electrified passenger trains. This led him to create a new design of steel passenger cars by 1912, and work with the Erie Railroad to create a fleet of passenger cars starting soon after. This car seats 92 and was purchased from the Kentucky Railway Museum.
2	Erie Railroad	This coach was built as Erie #2420 by Pullman in 1934. Known as a Stillwell car for its designer L.B. Stillwell, this car seats 92. The Whitewater Valley Railroad purchased the car from the Kentucky Railway Museum.

3	Erie Railroad	This Stillwell coach was built for longer suburban use and seats 76. It was built in 1934 by American Car & Foundry (ACF) as Erie #2634. The Whitewater Valley Railroad purchased the car from the Erie-Lackawanna Railroad and used it during the first year of operations.
4	Erie Railroad	This Stillwell coach was built for longer suburban use and seats 76. It was built in 1934 by American Car & Foundry (ACF) as Erie #2612. The Whitewater Valley Railroad purchased the car from the Erie-Lackawanna Railroad and used it during the first year of operations.
5	Erie Railroad	This Stillwell coach was built for longer suburban use and seats 76. It was built in 1934 by American Car & Foundry (ACF) as Erie #2600. The Whitewater Valley Railroad purchased the car from the Erie-Lackawanna Railroad and used it during the first year of operations.

6	Boston & Albany	This car has been used by a large number of passenger operators. It was used as Boston & Albany #1135 in commuter service, and then was transferred to the owner of the B&A, the New York Central. The car was sold several more times, being owned by the Delaware & Hudson, the New York, Susquehanna & Western (#212), and Cadillac & Lake City. The car seats 96.
7	Rock Island	This was Chicago, Rock Island & Pacific Railway #2528. It was built in 1923 by the Standard Steel Car Company, one of fifty for that order. Known as Al Capone Cars, they were retired and sold in the late 1970s. This car was purchased from the Illinois Railway Museum in 1985.
8	Erie Railroad	This former Stillwell commuter car, formerly Erie #2331, is five feet shorter than the rest of the Erie cars on the railroad. It seats 86 and was built in 1926 by the Pressed Steel Car Company. It is also unique in that it still has arches above the windows. The car later went to the Chicago & Western Indiana, and was purchased from the Marquette & Huron Mountain in 1985.

9	Chicago & North Western	Built as C&NW #7718, this car is unique in that it was built as a commuter combine with a passenger and freight section, designed to allow commuter trains to deliver newspapers and other similar parcel packages. The car was built by the American Car & Foundry and seats 70. It was purchased from the Marquette & Huron Mountain (#102) in 1985.
10	Rock Island	This was Chicago, Rock Island & Pacific Railway #2595. It was built in 1928 by the Standard Steel Car Company, one of fifty for the second order of steel commuter cars. Also known as Al Capone Cars, they were retired and sold in the late 1970s. This car was purchased from the Illinois Railway Museum in 1985. It seats 97.
7718	Chicago & North Western	This combination car – part coach and part baggage car – was built in 1923 by the American Car & Foundry company. It later was used by the Marquette & Huron Mountain as their #102. It came to the Whitewater Valley Railroad in 1985.
15481	Canadian National	This car was built as a steam generator car for the Canadian National. It later went to ViaRail in Canada, and then the Tuscola and Saginaw Bay Railway. The Whitewater Valley Railroad acquired it in 2010.

Equipment Roster

X4293	Baltimore & Ohio	This car was built as a baggage car. It was rebuilt into an express combine with a 15-foot mail apartment. It later became maintenance-of-way camp car #X4293. The car was donated to the Whitewater Valley Railroad by the Chessie System in 1986. In 1995, the car was sold to the B&O Railroad Museum, but is still stored in Connersville.
X4296	Pere Marquette	This car was built as a coach for the Pere Marquette, then later went to the Chesapeake & Ohio. It was converted into Baltimore & Ohio maintenance-of-way camp car #X4296. The car was donated to the Whitewater Valley Railroad by the Chessie System in 1986. In 1995, the car was sold to the B&O Railroad Museum, but is still stored in Connersville.
915113	Baltimore & Ohio	This car was built as a baggage car. It was converted into Baltimore & Ohio maintenance-of-way camp car #915113.

Rock Island coach 2595, Whitewater Valley Car 10, is commonly used on many regular trips. Photo by Barton Jennings.

Freight Cars

The Whitewater Valley Railroad also has a collection of freight cars that are used for photography events, educational displays, material storage, and for work along the railroad.

No.	Original Owner	Builder and History
6435	Railway Express Agency	This 40' boxcar is lettered as REX 6435 and was built in August 1930. The Railway Express Agency (REA) was a national small package and parcel network using railroads plus local delivery networks. It was created by the United States during World War I to consolidate and simplify the many regional networks that then existed. REA closed in 1975. This boxcar is not a real REA car, as cars in the REX 6100-6599 series were actually 50' express reefers that could also handle fresh fruits and vegetables. Instead, this car was originally Norfolk & Western 50017, built in 1930. It was used for heating passenger cars in winter until retired in 2010.
25009	Swift Refrigerator Line	This SRLX car is a 50-foot mechanical refrigerator built by General American in 1954.
25022	Swift Refrigerator Line	This SRLX car is a 50-foot mechanical refrigerator built by General American in 1954.

Equipment Roster

25044	Swift Refrigerator Line	This SRLX car is a 50-foot mechanical refrigerator built by General American in 1954.
25047	Swift Refrigerator Line	This SRLX car is a 50-foot mechanical refrigerator built by General American in 1954.
37214	Milwaukee Road	This is refrigerator car URTX, once owned by Union Refrigerator Transit Lines, which leased railroad freight cars to railroads and shippers.
56752	Canadian National	This side dump gondola was built in 1958 by National Steel Car. These cars can dump their load to the side using air pressure from the car's brake line.
63220	Virginian	This 50-ton boxcar was built in 1952 by Pullman-Standard at their Michigan City, Indiana, plant. The Virginian was a railroad that primarily hauled coal from West Virginia east to markets. It later became part of Norfolk & Western and then Norfolk Southern, which donated the car to the Whitewater Valley Railroad in 1990.

64370	Nickel Plate Road	This two-bay 50-ton open hopper was built by American Car & Foundry (ACF) in 1948. It was originally owned by the Wheeling & Lake Erie (W&LE) and was used to haul coal and similar products. The car went to the NKP in 1949 when the W&LE was leased. The Whitewater Valley Railroad acquired it in the 1990s and uses it to distribute rock ballast along the line.
91282	Baltimore & Ohio	This flatcar is a typical piece of equipment used to move large items by rail. This flatcar is often used to move rail for track work.
270113	Baltimore & Ohio	This is a 40-foot boxcar. Reportedly the railroad also has a second similar B&O boxcar.

???	???	This is a much older style of a side dump car, a car that can tilt to either side to unload materials, generally rock or stone for track embankment work. This car was purchased in 1995 from a quarry at Circleville, Ohio. It was built to very old standards with old K brakes and arch bar trucks, designs no longer allowed in regular freight service. The car was built by the Kilbourne & Jacobs Manufacturing Company, a manufacturer of bodies and semi-trailers for heavy service motor trucks, road and levee scrapers, excavating carts, wheelbarrows, and also these specialized railcars. According to the 1921 *Maintenance of Way Cyclopedia*, K&J was the "originator and pioneer builder of automatic two way, side dumping air dump cars." The first cars of this type were in service on the Carolina, Clinchfield and Ohio Railroad by 1908.

REX 6435 boxcar, Laurel. Photo by Barton Jennings.

While generally used as displays, the freight cars are sometimes used for photo charters. Photo by Barton Jennings.

Equipment Roster

Cabooses

The Whitewater Valley Railroad has an impressive collection of cabooses, especially wooden cabooses that once were used by the Baltimore & Ohio Railroad.

No.	Original Owner	Builder and History
521	Elgin, Joliet & Eastern	Known as a Way Car by the railroad, this all-steel caboose is believed to have been built in 1956 by the Morrison International Corporation at their Buffalo, New York, shop. The forty-foot caboose has a non-centered cupola. The caboose was at the Railroad Museum of Greater Cincinnati at Covington, Kentucky, and was later sold to the Whitewater Valley Railroad.
759	Nickel Plate Road	This steel cupola caboose was built by the Wheeling & Lake Erie's Ironton shops in late 1948 as #0259. It became Nickel Plate Road #759 with the acquisition of the W&LE later that year. Later it became Norfolk & Western #557759, and then became the property of Norfolk Southern, who donated it to the Whitewater Valley Railroad in 1990.
04946	Erie Railroad	This wooden caboose was used for years as the Metamora ticket station. It was built in 1929 by the Magor Car Company. It came to the Whitewater Valley Railroad in 1973.

18278	New York Central	This is an N9 class caboose. Used as a local transfer caboose, the design was approved by New York Central and construction began, with the last of the 160 cabooses (18195-18354) being completed by Penn Central. The Whitewater Valley Railroad has installed benches on the large end platforms for passengers.
18453	Penn Central	This is an N11 class caboose that was built by Penn Central at their Despatch Shops in East Rochester, New York. Built 1969-1970, this transfer caboose is 32 feet long, much shorter than the N9 class caboose. The crew cabin is the same size as the longer N9 cabooses, so the end platforms are much smaller.
90299	Chesapeake & Ohio	This steel cupola caboose, class C-20, was built in July 1949, by the American Car & Foundry. It was later sold to a private individual before coming to the Whitewater Valley in 2012.

Equipment Roster

C1902	Baltimore & Ohio	Caboose C-1902 was the second I-5 class caboose built at the B&O shops at Washington, Indiana. It is the oldest I-5 still remaining. The I-5 cabooses have a center cupola design, built with tongue and groove siding with steel ends and frame. The B&O built 272 Class I-5 cabooses 1924-1929 at both Washington and the shops at Mt. Clare, Maryland. Another 130 were manufactured at other locations. The last were retired in the early 1980s.
C2028	Baltimore & Ohio	This is another wooden, tongue and groove siding I-5 caboose.
C2125	Baltimore & Ohio	This is another wooden, tongue and groove siding I-5 caboose.
C2129	Baltimore & Ohio	This is a wooden, tongue and groove siding I-5D caboose. Early I-5 cabooses had a problem derailing when being pushed, reportedly caused by their short wheelbase. Classes I-5C and I-5D were lengthened, and had concrete floors to add weight. This caboose is painted Whitewater Valley Railroad.
C2232	Baltimore & Ohio	This is a wooden, tongue and groove siding I-5D caboose. Early I-5 cabooses had a problem derailing when being pushed, reportedly caused by their short wheelbase. Classes I-5C and I-5D were lengthened, and had concrete floors to add weight.

NKP 759 caboose, Connersville. Photo by Barton Jennings.

B&O C2028 caboose is posed next to Dearborn Tower at Connersville. Photo by Barton Jennings.

B&O caboose C2232 trails a Whitewater Limited train. Photo by Barton Jennings.

Each coach is marked with a number and a "Welcome Aboard" greeting. Photo by Sarah Jennings.

Route Guide of the Whitewater Valley Railroad

Because the Whitewater Valley Railroad operates passenger trains over almost its entire system for different events, this book will provide information about the entire line that the railroad owns, including the few miles north of the Connersville station that seldom see train operations. The guide covers the railroad from north to south, from Connersville to Metamora, just as most passengers first ride the line.

Directions on this railroad will be based upon the railroad's own terminology. A train heading from Connersville to Metamora is heading south, so to the left is railroad-east, and to the right is railroad-west. Because of the change in direction, and the fact that some passengers may be sitting backwards, the east and west direction will generally be used for the direction to look from the train.

Note that every station and bridge location is also identified by a milepost location. Railroads identify locations along their routes by mileposts, much like highways do. For the Whitewater Valley Railroad, the mileposts date back to the early days of the railroad and their distance from Cincinnati. There are signs every mile along the railroad that identify this distance. These signs are generally located on the east side of the tracks, so watch for them if you wish.

It should be noted that this guide is not designed to be a complete history of the railroad or a picture book, but instead includes a great deal of information for those who like to ask, "Where are we and what once happened here?" Because of this, the guide includes current as well as former station locations, historic towns, and major stream crossings along the line. An excellent companion to this book is *Images of Rail – Whitewater Valley Railroad* by Francis H. Parker and Judy Clem.

Many of the locations described are not official railroad stations, but are locations with a history related to the railroad or the earlier canal. Locations that are currently recognized by the Whitewater Valley Railroad are underlined.

69.4 CONNERSVILLE WEST 18TH STREET – Most of the importance of Connersville was due to a number of industries on the north side of Connersville, so they are included here to assist the reader in understanding the history of the town.

This area was a busy center of industry for Connersville, and once a center of automobile manufacturing. This explains why this part of the line was maintained when the line from Connersville south was abandoned. During the early part of the Twentieth Century, at least 13 different automobile lines were manufactured or assembled in Connersville. This caused Connersville to be called the "Little Detroit of Indiana." These cars included:

Car Name	Manufacturer	Assembly Dates
Ansted	Lexington Motor Car Co.	1921, 1926
Auburn	Auburn Automobile Co.	1929-36
Central	Central Manufacturing Co.	1905
Connersville	Connersville Motor Vehicle Co.	1906
Connersville	Connersville Buggy Co.	1914
Cord	Cord Corporation	1936-37
Empire	Empire Motor Car Co.	1912-15
Howard	Lexington-Howard Co.	1913-14
Lexington	Lexington Motor Co.	1910-27
McFarlan	McFarlan Motor Car Co.	1910-28
Pak-Age-Car	Auburn Central Co.	1938-41
Packard Darrin	Packard Motor Car Co.	1940-41
Van Auken Electric	Connersville Buggy Co.	1913

Information from several factory lists and maps, including the July 1919 Sanborn Map Company documents, showed that the area housed a number of factories and warehouses. The area north of West 18th Street, and to the west of the former canal, was once the home of the Lexington Motor Company, described by Sanborn as a "Mfg of Automobiles." Just to the east Sanborn showed the Central Motor Company, "Mfg of Automobile Bodies." A third plant in the area was the Indiana Lamp Company – "Mfg of Automobile Lamps."

The **Lexington Motor Company** was initially founded in 1909 in Lexington, Kentucky. A group of Connersville business leaders, desiring to diversify the manufacturing in the area, encouraged Lexington Motor to move to their community. The company located their headquarters at 1950 Columbia Avenue and built a series of assembly plants and buildings at 800 West 18th Street. The company was noted for John C. Moore's multiple exhaust design. New financial partners led the company to change its name to Lexington-Howard in 1913, and then back to Lexington Motor Company in 1915.

The company continued to expand, partnering with Ansted Engineering Company and their Teetor-Harley Motor Corporation of Hagerstown, Indiana. The result was a new engine factory in Connersville. The new partnership led to multiple wins in auto races such as the Pikes Peak Hill Climb. In 1920, Lexington Motor, Ansted Engineering Company, Connersville Foundry Corporation, and Teetor-Harley Motor Corporation were merged into the new United States Automotive Corporation. In that year, Lexington Motor produced more than 600 cars, its peak of production. The recession of the early 1920s hurt the company and it entered receivership. In 1927, the Lexington Motor Car Company was sold to the Auburn Automobile Company and soon shut down.

What Sanborn showed as the "Central Motor Company" was the **Central Manufacturing Company**, incorporated on April 7, 1898, to manufacture vehicle woodwork. In 1903, the firm built its first automobile body for Cadillac. The firm built one car in 1905, but the factory burned and the firm returned to building car bodies for other car companies at their new plant on 18th Street. Companies that used their bodies included Apperson, Auburn, Cole, Davis, Elcar, Empire, Gardner, National, Overland, Stutz, and Lexington. In May 1930, the Central Manufacturing Company plant was sold to the Auburn Automobile Company.

A third plant in this complex was the **Indiana Lamp Company**, started by Mr. Ansted in 1904 to manufacture lamps for automobiles and other uses. This allowed Ansted to control the manufacture of almost every part needed for his Lexington and other cars.

69.2 CLAYPOOL'S LOCK (#43) – This lock, designated as Lock #43, was located at what is today 16th Street and Illinois Avenue. The name Claypool comes from the Claypool family. Newton and Solomon Claypool were involved with the start of the canal, and Solomon Claypool was a director of the canal company at the time of the completion of the canal to Cambridge City. Newton and Solomon Claypool arrived in the Connersville area in 1817. They traded with local Indians for a few years before Solomon began farming while Newton opened a tavern and hotel.

To the east of the railroad was another area that was part of the automobile manufacturing industry in Connersville. One of these was the **Wainwright Engineering Company**, a manufacturer of engines and engine parts. The firm was started by William Warren Wainwright in 1903. The firm built the first engine for the McFarlan automobile. The firm also built farm tractors and parts for the 155 mm Howitzer artillery guns. The firm was sold to McQuay-Norris Manufacturing of St. Louis on December 11, 1921.

To the south of the Wainwright facility and just north of the Connersville City Cemetery was the **Rex Manufacturing Company** – "Mfg Auto Bodies & Tops." The Rex Buggy Manufacturing Company was founded in 1898 and purchased the Munk & Roberts Furniture Company factory to build horse-drawn buggies and light carriages, sold as Rex and Yale products. The firm quickly moved into automobile products, and manufactured convertible and all-weather tops for several automobile firms. The company also manufactured aftermarket bodies for the Ford Model T during the mid-Twenties. During this time, some of the executives of Rex were also executives or directors of the Central Manufacturing Company and Lexington Motor Company.

To the west of the railroad were more plants, switched by both the Cleveland, Cincinnati, Chicago & St. Louis (CCC&StL) and Cincinnati, Indianapolis & Western (CI&W). North of Mount Street and along and east of Columbia Avenue was **The Standard Parts Company**, also known as the Ansted Spring & Axle Division. This firm built parts for several car manufacturers in the area. While the term "manufacturer" is used, most of the automobile companies actually bought parts from multiple companies and then assembled them into a car with their name.

Just north of today's CSX elevated line and south of Mount Street was the **McFarlan Motor Company**, identified by Sanborn as a manufacturer of automobiles. The firm started as the McFarlan Carriage Company, which was founded by John B. McFarlan in 1856. Alfred Harry McFarlan, the grandson of John B. McFarlan, moved the firm into the automobile business. The first car was built in 1910. The McFarlan was a luxury car, known as the "American Rolls Royce." It was popular with celebrities and politicians such as actor Fatty Arbuckle, director William Desmond Taylor, boxer Jack Dempsey, and crime boss Al Capone. Although the cars were popular, sales were small and the firm entered bankruptcy in 1928 and built its last car that year.

Just west of the McFarlan facility was **The Connersville Blower Company**, a manufacturer of rotary blowers and pumps. In 1931, Connersville Blower merged with Roots Blower to become the Roots-Connersville Blower Company.

There were some non-automobile companies in this area. The **Connersville Furniture Company**, once located north of Mount Street, was organized in February 1882. It built its factory on the site of a burned coffin company. The factory was located on the banks of the Whitewater Canal for its power. The first furniture manufactured was black walnut bedroom suites. The firm expanded and was soon making furniture for John Wanamaker and Marshall Field's, two major department store chains. They also received contracts to make radio cabinets for a dozen different distribution firms. The firm entered receivership on April 6, 1927. The McQuay-Norris Company, which manufactured specialized machine parts, bought one of the buildings in 1929. The original factory building became the Connersville Cabinet Company, but it failed in late 1931. It then became a casket factory, but sold out to McQuay-Norris on December 30, 1933. During the 1950s, the Roots-Connersvilie Blower Company purchased the building.

Also located in this area was the **Hydro-Electric Light & Power Company**. This facility used a flume under the building from a head race to the west of the plant back to the canal. The plant also received coal from the railroad, creating steam for several generators. The electric company had a contract with the City of Connersville to provide power for the community, and commenced operations in 1911. In 1917, a second firm was merged into the power company.

To reach all of the industries to the west of the canal, the Whitewater Valley Railroad had a bridge across the canal at the east end of Mount Street. The railroad had a tool house here on the west side of tracks just north of the bridge. There was also a spur track to the east alongside the mainline.

While many of the buildings still stand from this era, the companies are mostly gone. The last major automobile parts manufacturer, Visteon, closed its plant at Connersville in 2007. The plant had been operated by Ford previously, but the auto slump led to its sale and then closure. In this area today are several industries. North of the cemetery is Reclaimed Energy Inc., a company that recycles waste solvents. Where the McFarlan Motor Company once built cars is Howden Roots, which manufactures rotary positive displacement blowers and centrifugal compressors, modern versions of the early Roots Blowers. Just to the north is Stant, a company founded in 1898 that became the world's largest producer of piano tuning pins. Today, Stant is a manufacturer of vapor management systems, on-board vapor recovery components, fuel delivery systems, thermal management systems, and similar engineered products. Also in this area are several warehouses used to distribute store fixtures and other business fixtures.

69.0 **IH JUNCTION** – IH Junction was once the connection with the Indiana Hi-Rail railroad. This location, the north end of the Whitewater Valley Railroad, is easy to find as it is at the north end of track, located just south of the connecting track between CSX and the Big Four Terminal Railroad (BFTR) near West 12th Street. The Big Four Terminal Railroad reached an agreement to operate the 5.2 miles of track between Connersville and Beesons owned by RMW Ventures, LLC. The line had previously been operated by the C&NC Railroad, known by some as the Connersville & New Castle Railroad (CNUR). The C&NC began operations on December 22, 1997, operating the former Indiana Hi-Rail line north to New Castle. The Indiana Hi-Rail began operating the line during December 1981. The C&NC Railroad still operates the line between Beesons and a connection with Norfolk Southern at New Castle, a total of almost 28 miles.

To the west along Illinois Avenue is a reminder of the manufacturing history of Connersville. Used since 2015 as the Pattern Mill Senior Housing Project, this building is the former Connersville Furniture Company building, or Roots Pattern Shop. This six-story building is a beautiful reminder of the history of Connersville.

The Roots Pattern Shop is today the Pattern Mill Senior Housing Project, located to the west of the railroad. Photo by Sarah Jennings.

68.8 **MILL LOCK (#42)** – Located on the southwest side of City Cemetery was Lock #42. There is no sign of this lock today.

In this area is a historic railroad tell-tale, a structure that was once quite common along railroad tracks. It was used to warn railroad brakemen, who rode the top of freight cars to manually operate the freight car brakes, that a low obstruction was ahead. These obstructions could include things like a tunnel entrance, water tower, signal, or bridge structure. A tell-tale featured ropes that hung down from an overhead bar which would alert a brakemen to these risks.

A WWV volunteer demonstrates the purpose of a tell-tale during a special event. Photo by Barton Jennings.

68.7 CSXT OVERPASS – Overhead is the CSX Indianapolis Subdivision of the Louisville Division. This line connects Cincinnati, Ohio, with Indianapolis, Indiana. Just east of the overpass is the Connersville Yard and the Connersville Amtrak passenger station. The Amtrak station is a 3-sided brick shelter built by Connersville in a style similar to the original station. The Amtrak station is used by the *Cardinal*, trains #50 (from Chicago to New York via Washington, DC) and #51 (New York to Chicago via Washington, DC). Each train operates three days per week and passes through Connersville in the middle of the night, as of 2018. Next to the Amtrak station is the original brick station, built by the Cincinnati, Indianapolis & Western Railroad in 1914. CSX maintenance-of-way (track and bridge maintenance and engineering) forces currently use the building.

A CSX freight passes over WWV 25 at the overpass in Connersville. Photo by Barton Jennings.

The former Cincinnati, Indianapolis & Western Railroad depot stands east of the CSX overhead bridge. Photo by Barton Jennings.

The CSX line dates back to the Junction Railroad Company, which was incorporated on February 15, 1848, to build a railroad from Rushville, Indiana, to the southeast to Hamilton, Ohio. At Hamilton, the railroad would connect with the Cincinnati, Hamilton & Dayton Railroad, and the Atlantic & Great Western Railroad. In February 1853, the Ohio & Indianapolis Railroad Company (O&I)

was incorporated to build the line west of Rushville. In April of the same year, the O&I was merged into the Junction Railroad Company. By 1864, the railroad was completed between Hamilton and Connersville, a total of 42 miles, and the 56 miles west to Indianapolis was almost completed. The Junction Railroad Company was sold to the Cincinnati, Hamilton & Indianapolis Railroad Company (CH&I) at foreclosure on January 2, 1878.

The CH&I merged with the Indiana, Decatur & Western Railway Company to form the Cincinnati, Indianapolis & Western Railway Company in September 1902. It was sold at foreclosure to the Cincinnati, Indianapolis & Western Railroad Company (CI&W) on October 30, 1915. In 1927, the CI&W was acquired by the Baltimore and Ohio Railroad (B&O). In 1963, the B&O was acquired by the Chesapeake & Ohio Railway (C&O). In 1973, the B&O, C&O, and the Western Maryland Railway created the Chessie System to coordinate their operations. CSX Corporation was created in 1980 to consolidate the management of a number of railroads. The B&O was merged into CSX Transportation on August 31, 1987, ending the corporate existence of the first common carrier railroad in the United States.

In 1919, the area east of the overpass and west of the Whitewater River was a significant station on the railroad. The Cincinnati, Indianapolis & Western Railroad had a freight depot on the northeast corner of East 10th Street and Eastern Avenue. To the north of the tracks and on the east side of Eastern Avenue, between 10th and 11th Streets, was the CI&W passenger station, one of the few Connersville railroad structures that still stand. There was a small yard between the two railroad buildings. East of the passenger depot, there was a turntable and 2-stall roundhouse, plus several other yard structures such as a water tower and coal shed. Also in this area was the junction with the Lake Erie & Western Railroad.

Lake Erie & Western Railroad

The Lake Erie & Western Railroad (LE&W) started as the Fremont & Indiana Railroad Company on April 22, 1853, with the goal of building a route from Fremont, Ohio, southwest towards the Indiana State line. Over the next few decades, the company acquired a number of other connecting lines, becoming a part of the Lake Erie & Western. The LE&W created the Connersville & New Castle Junction Railroad Company on October 23, 1863, to build a line north from Connersville. The line reached Cambridge City in April 1865, and then New Castle in 1867. It was merged with the New Castle & Muncie Rail Road Company on January 2, 1868, becoming the Cincinnati, Connersville & Muncie Rail Road Company. This line was extended north, reaching Muncie in February 1869. Through several more mergers, the line was extended north to Fort Wayne. The line became part of the LE&W in 1890, and on July 1, 1922, the Nickel Plate Road. Between Connnersville and Cambridge City, the LE&W and the CCC&StL lines were almost side-by-side and eventually the New York Central agreed to use the Nickel Plate route between Beesons and Cambridge City in 1931. On October 16, 1964, the Nickel Plate became part of Norfolk & Western, which merged with Southern Railway in the early 1980s to form Norfolk Southern. The five miles of track from Connersville to Beesons, part of the Connersville Branch, was abandoned by Norfolk Southern in 1988.

At one time, the Lake Erie & Western cooperated with the Indianapolis, Cincinnati & Lafayette and the Big Four by operating a through parlor car service between Cincinnati and Fort Wayne via the connection at Connersville. Through cars to Indianapolis and Chicago once operated over the line, giving Connersville an excellent selection of passenger services.

Indianapolis & Cincinnati Traction

From 1906 until 1932, Connersville had a fourth railroad – the Indianapolis & Cincinnati Traction Company. During the late 1800s and early 1900s, thousands of miles of electric interurban railroads were built across the country. This was due to several new technologies which allowed long-distance electrical transmission systems, and smaller but more powerful electric motors. Indiana, known as the Interurban Capitol of the World, at its peak had 111 different interurban companies operating over 2000 miles of track. Every major city but Evansville had a line that reached Indianapolis.

One of these railroads was the Indianapolis & Cincinnati Traction. The line started as the Indianapolis, Shelbyville & Southeastern Traction Company in late 1901, and was sold to the Indianapolis & Cincinnati Traction Company on October 13, 1903. In 1905, the line reached Rushville, and in 1906, the interurban company expanded the system by building a line east to Connersville as a part of the plans to reach Cincinnati. This line was unique in that it used Westinghouse single-phase AC (alternating current) electrification as opposed to the more typical DC (direct current) electrification. The railroad went bankrupt in 1906, and was sold through foreclosure on November 14, 1910, but it kept the same name. The company rebuilt the system with conventional 600-volt DC in 1923, bought new equipment, and went into receivership over the next few years. In April 1928, the railroad was sold again, becoming the Indianapolis & Southeastern Railroad Company. On January 14, 1932, all train operations ended and buses took over the routes.

The line to Connersville was described in the October 12, 1907, issue of *Street Railway Journal*. It was described as rough country, with the need for a concrete arch bridge and a 900-foot fill over Williams Creek at Glenwood. The article noted that the route from Rushville to Connersville was three miles shorter than the competing steam route, which looped north to avoid the rough terrain. The article commented on the 66-foot-wide private right-of-way of the Connersville Extension, as well as the relatively heavy 70# rail used in the construction.

The electric line came into Connersville from the southwest, passing through the south edge of today's Willowbrook Country Club, to near 10th and Oak Streets. The line then followed 10th Street into town. The Indianapolis & Cincinnati Traction had their station on the southwest corner of East 6th and Water Streets. The line's freight house was immediately to the southwest.

68.7 **GRAND AVENUE** – The railroad crosses Grand Avenue, originally known as Market Avenue, a major north-south street through Connersville. Old maps show that just north of here, Western Avenue had tracks and the remains of the "hydraulic canal" in the center median.

Milepost 68.7 has been shown to be the milepost for Connersville in employee timetables for many years. A 38-car length (based upon 44-foot cars) siding once existed at Connersville, stretching from here south to just north of West 3rd Street, or as originally known, High Street.

68.6 **CONNERSVILLE LOCK (#41)** – Lock #41 was located about one block north of the railroad's downtown station, near North 6th Street, originally known as Head Street. There was also a canal basin in this area to hold barges serving local shippers.

68.5 **CONNERSVILLE STATION** – Located just south of 5th Street and on the east side of the tracks is the new Connersville station used by the Whitewater Valley Railroad, built in 1997 and promoted as "Grand Central Station" by the community. The station features a waiting room and ticket office, a gift shop, and many displays about the area's history. Note the DSS&A benches inside. These are from the Duluth, South Shore & Atlantic Railway, obtained in an auction in 1985. The DSS&A operated from Sault Ste.

Marie, Michigan, west to Duluth, Minnesota, providing service along the Lake Superior shoreline of Wisconsin and throughout the Upper Peninsula of Michigan.

The Whitewater Valley Railroad operates out of this modern station in Connersville, Indiana. Photo by Sarah Jennings.

The new station sits where the Cleveland, Cincinnati, Chicago & St. Louis (CCC&StL) wood frame Freight Depot stood until the 1970s. Just across the tracks was once the CCC&StL Passenger Depot, also wood frame, which was built over the canal on the south side of 5th Street, originally Harrison Street. It was torn down by 1953. There was a separate baggage room to the south. A siding was located on the east side of the mainline to serve the freight depot. The train stations along this line all used a similar design. They were one story with vertical board and batten wood siding, with agent quarters under the roof line. Large windows on each end of the building provided light for this upper level.

As with the area around many railroad stations, there were a number of railroad-related and civic buildings nearby. In 1919, a block to the north was the Connersville Lumber Company planing mill, with the four-story McFarlan Hotel to its east. Just east of the freight depot was the three-story Grand Hotel. The J. F. Carlos Feed Mill was located just south of the freight depot and north of West 4th Street. To the east of the mill was the City Hall, Central Fire Station, and Masonic Lodge (all one building). The Fayette County Court House was just east of this building. The court house building was built in 1890 and included parts of the original 1849 building. The southeast corner includes a circular corner clock tower topped by a steep conical spire. The building has been expanded to the west to include the land upon which the former city hall stood, and the entire structure was placed on the National Register of Historic Places in 2006.

The City of Connersville

Connersville was founded in 1808 when John Conner established an Indian trading post on the West Fork of the Whitewater River. He and his brother William had earlier settled about twenty miles south of here in 1802. This earlier location was known as Cedar Grove, and later as Conner's Post. Conner chose the new location because of the large number of old trails which crossed in this area. Conner officially acquired the land in the area in 1811 and later platted the town in 1813. Conner was the first sheriff, operated the first sawmill, tavern and store in the area. In 1816, he became the first state senator from the area. In 1820, he was one of nine commissioners who located Indianapolis as the new state capital. In 1825, John Conner was selected to receive General Lafayette during his visit and tour of the United States. Conner died in 1826 while a member of the House of Representatives.

Due to the amount of area timber, the good transportation, and the large number of skilled craftsmen, a great deal of industry soon developed in the area. The first businesses included a general store, a distillery, a sawmill, and a gristmill. The town received an added boost when it was selected as the county seat of the new Fayette County. The Connersville post office opened in January, 1818, and the courthouse was finished by 1822. The *Indiana Statesman* newspaper started publishing in 1824. By 1833, the population was 500, and Connersville was incorporated in 1841.

The White Water Valley Canal reached here in 1845, the Junction Railroad Company in 1862, and the White Water Railroad in 1865. Many of the first industries in the area involved woodworking, giving Connersville the identity of a furniture and buggy town. Connersville was also the location of early automotive manufacturing, including companies such as Auburn, Lexington, McFarland, Cord and Empire. Connersville became famous when McFarland Carriage Company manufactured the first medium priced 6-cylinder automobile in the U.S. in 1909. Because of the number of factories, the population of Connersville was 9000 by 1919. The large number of auto and auto parts factories that sprang up in the area caused Connersville to sometimes be proclaimed "Little Detroit." Most are today closed but a few auto parts factories still exist on the north side of town.

Today, Connersville has a population of less than 15,000. It is still the county seat of Fayette County, the largest and only incorporated town in the county. It is also the home of the only high school in the county.

68.3 WEST 2ND STREET – This area was once very busy for the railroad, and the street was known as Baltimore Street. The area to the east of the tracks is the location of the original New York Central service facilities in Connersville. It featured a water tank, sand house, and a turntable for turning commuter trains from Cincinnati. In 1951, the railroad's employee timetable listed a siding, scale track, station, turntable, and an engine watchman's cabin at Connersville.

South of West 1st Street, or Short Street, the railroad once crossed over a Hydraulic Canal connecting the White Water Canal with the Whitewater River. This was once the feeder canal from the Connersville Feeder Dam. The Hydro-Electric Light & Power Company artificial gas plant was further to the south, located south of Springhill Avenue. It was served by a spur track to the east and was identified as being vacant in a 1919 Sanborn map.

68.1 **CONWELL LOCK (#40)** – This was Lock #40, located just south of the Feeder Canal connection north of South 1st Street. The Feeder Canal flowed in from the Feeder Dam on the Whitewater River to the east.

Several members of the Conwell family were active in the area, including A. B., James, William, and Isaac. Records of the times show them all to be merchants and successful businessmen. James Conwell was involved with the founding of the community of Laurel to the south. His brother A. B. had first gone to Pittsburgh, and then to Connersville by 1821. In this area, A. B. Conwell owned a tannery, a pork processing facility, and a flour mill. Later the firm was known as A. B. Conwell & Sons, and was noted as proprietors of Conwell Mills.

In 1868, Abraham Conwell sued the White Water Valley Canal Company, the Connersville Hydraulic Company, the White Water Valley Railroad Company, and twelve other defendants. The suit involved access to the water from the Whitewater River, something that Abraham Conwell stated that he and his farm were being denied. The suit was based upon the canal having water rights only for navigation. However, the suit was dismissed due to laws passed to allow the transfer of the canal property to other purposes.

68.0 **PORK HOUSE LOCK (#39)** – The few remains of Lock #39 are immediately to the west of the tracks. This lock received its name from Conwell's Pork House processing facility that once stood nearby.

Route Guide

Pork House Lock (Lock #39) stands next to the tracks to the west, but is hard to see from the train. Photo by Barton Jennings.

67.9 **SOUTH CONNERSVILLE YARD** – This is the north end of the yard complex used by the Whitewater Valley Railroad.

67.8 **SWITCH** – Located next to South End Auto scrap yard, once the site of the 20th Century Mixer Company, this switch connected to an industry track that looped through the various plants to the east and headed north to serve several more industries. There were also a number of industries here, located on several other spur tracks to the east. These included the Connersville Ice Company ice plant, J. Kooh's Slaughter House, and the P. H. and F. M. Roots Warehouse. The long industry track looped back north as far as East 2nd Street. Here the line reached the Valley Roller Mills of the UHL Snider Milling Company, located along the Whitewater River.

Just to the south of the roller mill was the large manufacturing complex of **P. H. and F. M. Roots Company**, shown by Sanborn as "Mfg Rotary Pressure Blowers, Rotary Pumps, Forges, etc." The Roots Company was created in 1859 by Philander Higley Roots and Francis Marion Roots. The brothers built a mill here, and while experimenting to make it more efficient, discovered that their system could push enough air to blow a hat off someone. The superintendent of a local iron foundry commented that the system could be used to create higher temperatures in a foundry. With the idea, the brothers created the Roots Blower.

In 1860, the Roots brothers patented the Roots Blower, and obtained an international patent in 1869 for "improvements in rotary blowing machines." By 1875, the system was also being used to provide ventilation in mines. The big boost to the Connersville firm was the invention of the automobile. In 1900, Gottlieb Daimler patented a Roots supercharger for an internal combustion engine. Other new products came along, such as the centrifugal compressor in 1931. The same year, the firm was acquired by the International Derrick and Equipment Company and merged with the Connersville Blower Company to become the Roots-Connersville Blower Company. World War II caused the firm to add submarine screw compressors, systems to blow ballast water, to their list of products. Today, Roots Blowers are mainly used as air pumps in superchargers for internal combustion engines.

To the south of the Roots plant was another large industry, but one not associated with the automobile industry. This was the Werner Industries Company, located on both sides of Eastern Avenue north of Spring Hill Avenue. The railroad had a track to serve a coal storage facility at the boiler house. The magazine *Hardwood Record*, dated October 10, 1917, reported that, "The Krell Auto Grand Piano Company, Connersville, Ind., is now the Werner Industries Company of Cincinnati." Werner built a number of brands of pianos here, including Krell, Auto-Player, Duchess and Royal. Werner was acquired by The Starr Piano Company in 1927. Krell pianos were being built by Starr as late as 1950.

The John Ringloff slaughter house and stock pens were further to the south and along the Whitewater River.

67.7 WHITEWATER VALLEY SHOPS – To the east is the current headquarters and shop complex of the railroad, located in what was once the home of the Connersville Gravel Company. To the west is the current rail yard for the Whitewater Valley Railroad. This area is full of historic railroad equipment, many restored or being restored by volunteers of the railroad. For the history of some of the equipment, please see the Whitewater Valley Railroad Equipment Roster on Page 27.

The Whitewater Valley Railroad opened a new shop recently, improving their restoration efforts. Photo by Barton Jennings.

To the west is Elmhurst, the home of Warren Lodge #15, F&AM, since 1941. The building was originally built in 1831 by Congressman Oliver Hampton Smith, and it has served as a private home (1831-1902), a sanitarium and nursing home (1902-1909), and a girl's school (1909-1928) before being restored to its present design and use. A number of notable people can be traced to the structure. Samuel Parker, president of the Whitewater Canal, is included in the long list of one-time owners, as well as James Huston (U.S. Treasurer under President Benjamin Harrison) and Caleb Blood Smith (the person who seconded Lincoln's nomination at the Republican Convention). Mrs. Barry Goldwater attended school here. The house was added to the National Register of Historic Places in 1977.

To the west is Elmhurst, which once housed a school attended by Mrs. Barry Goldwater. Photo by Sarah Jennings.

67.4 WHITEWATER VALLEY RAILROAD DISPLAY AREA – Located just north of Indiana Highway 1, known locally as Veterans Memorial Drive, is the south end of the rail yard and shop complex of the Whitewater Valley Railroad. This is the planned display area for the railroad. Plans include a roundhouse with turntable, equipment display barn, car shop, and many other structures that are designed to represent a typical railroad shop complex from the early 1900s. Already located here is the former New York Central/Baltimore & Ohio Dearborn Tower from Lawrenceburg, Indiana, and the former Baltimore & Ohio depot from Rushville, Indiana.

Route Guide

The Dearborn Tower, built in 1896, was retired by CSXT in 1986 and moved here in 2003. The tower once protected the crossing between the Baltimore & Ohio's St. Louis Division mainline between St. Louis and Cincinnati, and the New York Central's Aurora Branch. The tower was no longer needed after the Aurora Branch was abandoned and new signals were installed by CSX, which operated the former B&O line. It is appropriate that this tower once protected the Cleveland, Cincinnati, Chicago & St. Louis Railroad (the Big Four, later New York Central), as that is the same railroad that operated the Whitewater Valley Railroad.

Former New York Central/Baltimore & Ohio Dearborn Tower, Connersville. Photo by Barton Jennings.

Towers such as this were once found along many railroads, especially where railroads crossed at grade. They were used to control train movements, to issue orders and authorize the movement of trains, and to ensure the safety of train operations. At the time of its preservation, it was believed that it was one of only eight existing tower structures in Indiana, and was the first to be preserved in eastern Indiana. It still has its manual controls and is being restored to its original condition. The tower is believed to have been the last manual interlocking tower in service in Indiana.

In 2008, the former B&O depot from Rushville, Indiana, was moved to the site. This move involved several years of planning and work, but the depot is a typical wooden depot of the region. Built by the Cincinnati, Hamilton & Dayton Railroad, the station is from the line that runs east-west across the Whitewater Valley Railroad just north of the Connersville station.

Dearborn Tower and Rushville Station are the first two structures moved to the planned Whitewater Valley Railroad display area. Photo by Sarah Jennings.

67.1 HERRON'S LOCK (#38) – Heading south, the railroad follows the route of the original Whitewater Canal all the way to Metamora. Some of the locks are easy to see while others have no remains, but they are marked by large brown signs. All of the locks were built to Erie Canal standards and thus were 15 feet wide and 90 feet long. The canal itself was 26 feet wide at the bottom and 40 feet wide at the top with a minimum water depth of 4 feet.

A lock is a system used to raise or lower a boat. For a boat to climb, it would enter the lock from the lower end with the upper gates closed. The lower gates would then be closed and water from the upper level would be allowed to slowly enter the lock, generally through several small valves, sluices or doors. When the water level was raised to the level of the canal above the lock, the upper gates could be opened and the barge pulled out of the lock. During the mid-1800s, the process was all done by hand and could take some time. However, speed wasn't a big issue as the barge itself was generally pulled along the canal by a horse or mule at walking speed.

The locks used miter gates, the traditional gates consisting of two leaves (gates). Miter gates, also spelled mitre, were invented by Leonardo da Vinci, sometime around the late 15th century. When closed, the gates meet at an angle like a chevron pointing upstream. When the upstream level is higher, even by a small amount, there is pressure on the gates that forces them together, sealing the gap between them. Miter gates can only be operated after water levels on each side have been equalized. Even when both gates are miter gates, they are not identical. The lower gates are taller, equaling the upper gate plus the rise of the lock. When the miter gates are open to allow a boat to pass, they are housed in a recess in the lock wall, requiring that the lock wall be longer than the lock itself.

Little remains of this lock. The lock was #38, also known as Herron's Lock, or Heron's Lock. James Herron was born in Baltimore, Maryland, and his parents moved to Indiana in 1837, buying the Claypool farm and tavern. This farm was located on the south side of Connersville alongside the West Fork Whitewater River. Herron was educated at Oxford College in Ohio, and began to operate businesses in the area. James Herron was a supporter of the canal, and he became the canal company's secretary and treasurer in 1845. Because of his position with the company and the fact that his family farm was nearby, Lock #38 was named for him. After the canal closed and it was used for hydraulic power, this was the south end of the Connersville service.

James Herron later was involved with railroads, helping to survey, locate and engineer both the Junction Railroad and the Whitewater Valley Railroad. He was also involved with the pork-packing industry in Connersville, especially the George Frybarger & Company; Caldwell, McCollem & Company; and the White Water Caldwell Pork-Packing Company. In 1862, the Fayette County Hog-Slaughtering & Pork-Packing Association was created with James Herron as its secretary. However, competition from other locations and the ability to move pork across the country by rail caused a failure of the Connersville companies, with all pork-packing closed by 1874.

Not far south of the location of Lock #38 is a grade crossing for Robinson's Whitewater River Campground. The campground sits between the railroad and the Whitewater River to the east. Recently IBCX caboose #502 has been moved here and is just east of the tracks. The bay window caboose was originally built for the Toledo, Peoria & Western Railway, and was stored at Beesons, Indiana, for more than a decade.

The road to the west is Indiana Highway 121, which generally follows the railroad closely until Laurel. The railroad will pass a number of small towns and farms on its way south.

TP&W caboose #502 can be seen to the east of the train as it passes the Robinson's Whitewater Campground. Photo by Sarah Jennings.

66.5 IRVING MATERIALS, INC. CROSSING – Located to the east is one of several old suppliers of stone and gravel along the route. Irving Materials, Inc. (IMI) dates back to 1946 when C. C. "Skunk" Irving started selling stone and cement in Greenfield, Indiana. The company now operates facilities across Indiana, and has four regional operational centers serving six different states. This facility produces stone, gravel and sand for local customers. They also produce track ballast for the Whitewater Valley Railroad.

65.6 UPDEGRAFT'S LOCK (#37) – Known as Lock #37, a bit of the lock is still visible in the woods between the tracks and the adjacent highway to the west. This lock, like most of the ones on this canal, is known as a composite lock. This means that it was built of rough-cut stone that was mortared together. Then the lock was lined with timber to protect the boats passing through it. This design was cheaper to build than a lock with smooth-cut stone. Stone was used on almost all locks because of the ample supply along the route. The lock has deteriorated greatly and no longer sits in water.

There are few records of the name, but Updegraft was a member of the House of Representatives of the State of Ohio during the construction of the canal.

65.2 WILLIAMS CREEK BRIDGE – Williams Creek forms near Bentonville, Indiana, northwest of Connersville, and flows to the south until it enters into the West Fork Whitewater River just downstream of this bridge. The first mills in the Connersville area were built on Williams Creek, with the first being James Reed's gristmill near here in 1814. Other mills owned by John Vance, John Hughes, James Brownlee and others were along the stream by 1820. Sawmills also were built along the creek to cut timber for area homes and businesses. There were several families in the area named Williams, so the creek was probably named for one of them.

The bridge that the railroad uses to cross Williams Creek is very unique. It consists of a pair of arch through plate girder spans, one of a few, if not the only railroad bridge of this design still in service. Each span is 99 feet long and was installed in 1917. It is known as a twin-arch bridge by the railroad, and as the Two Arch Bridge by many locals. This bridge was known as Bridge #139A by the New York Central.

The White Water Valley Canal Company built their Williams Creek Aqueduct here. The area is still a popular summer swimming hole, with often dozens of locals cooling off in Williams Creek and the Whitewater River.

WWV 25 heads south, crossing Williams Creek using a pair of arch through plate girder spans. Photo by Sarah Jennings.

64.8 **FALL CREEK BRIDGE** – Known as Three Mile Bridge, or railroad Bridge #139, this is a through plate girder bridge. Fall Creek starts on the west side of Fayette County and flows east into the West Fork Whitewater River just east of here.

64.4 **NULLTOWN LOCK (#36)** – The railroad at this location is basically on top of the canal and former Lock #36. The short grade here is the second steepest on the railroad. It was needed to get over the lock, showing that much of this line was simply thrown down on the existing right-of-way without much heavy engineering. The lock was named for nearby Nulltown, Indiana.

Just north of the lock is Chicken Farm Crossing, the nickname for a road crossing that once led to a farm where fighting gamecocks were raised.

64.2 POT CREEK BRIDGE – This creek forms about five miles to the west from a small series of streams that drain several farms. The short deck plate girder span was known as Bridge #137. Heading north, trains face a 1.02% grade.

63.9 NULLTOWN – Nulltown, spelled Null Town on some early maps, is located on the Whitewater River. It was also served by the White Water Canal and later the railroad. The area near Nulltown was settled at least by 1812 when a blockhouse was built to protect area settlers from Indian attacks during the War of 1812. The name Nulltown came about because William and Israel Null operated a sawmill here. The name Null's Mill was first used when the post office moved from nearby Ashland to here on February 26, 1847. It later took the name Nulltown.

The presence of the canal expanded the market for area products, and the Null brothers expanded their sawmill to include a flouring and gristmill. Later when the railroad was built, there was a siding to the east at Nulltown, as well as some stock pens and a grain elevator just to the east of the general store. Today, Nulltown is a small unincorporated community in Columbia Township of Fayette County.

63.6 WEST COUNTY ROAD 480S – This road is also known as County Road 80. It heads east and has a bridge that crosses the West Fork Whitewater River. To the west is a small mobile home community, the Green Acres Mobile Home Park.

On the east side of the tracks just south of the grade crossing is the Nulltown "International" Airport. The area is known for the Nulltown Wingnuts, a group of pilots who fly ultralight airplanes. They sponsor an annual fly-in every September into the small airfield to the east. The term "international" is used since the event draws air enthusiasts even from outside the United States.

Route Guide

A freight special is photographed from the adjacent airport runway. Photo by Barton Jennings.

63.1 BERLIN LOCK (#35) – The Berlin Lock was also known as Lock #35. Parts of this lock are clearly visible immediately to the west of the tracks. This stone lock was built using rough-cut stone and was lined with timber. It has greatly deteriorated and the canal has been mostly filled in through this area.

The name Berlin came from the name of a small community that once existed near here. In 1838, Dr. Philip Mason owned land in this area that he surveyed to create a town on the new canal. On October 29, 1838, he officially recorded the plat for the town of Berlin. However, Berlin had a short life as a village with only a few stores, all of which soon moved north to Nulltown or south to Alpine. The town was gone before the Civil War.

It should be noted that Dr. Mason had earlier been involved with Allen Crisler of nearby Alpine. In fact, it is reported that Mason had traded his farm for Crisler's sawmill in late 1816. However, the parties again swapped their properties in 1818.

The Berlin Lock is clearly visible as it is passed by the train. Photo by Sarah Jennings.

Many of the locks along the railroad are clearly marked, such as Lock #35, the Berlin Lock. Photo by Sarah Jennings.

62.9 **INDIANA HIGHWAY 121** – Heading south, Highway 121 curves across the tracks, moving from the west side of the line to the east. Indiana Highway 121 closely follows the railroad from Connersville south to just west of Metamora. The highway is only nineteen miles long and is broken into two parts. This is the southern fifteen miles, once designated as Indiana Highway 1. The northern part is located on the east side of Richmond, Indiana.

Heading south, the railroad and highway are right next to each other to Alpine. This area is a mix of farmland and pasture. To the east are some nice views across farmland of the Whitewater River and the low ridges on the far side of the stream.

61.9 **INDIANA HIGHWAY 121** – Highway 121 again crosses the tracks, moving from the east to the west side of the railroad heading south. South of Alpine, the railroad and highway separate for several miles. However, the railroad and river are side-by-side in this area, and the track has had the name "Alpine Straight."

61.8 <u>**ALPINE**</u> – Heading south, the railroad comes alongside the Whitewater River in this area. Alpine is a small rural community, located between the Whitewater River and a series of rolling hills. The first sawmill in the area was built here in 1814 by Allen Crisler. Crisler and Joshua Crigler arrived here in late 1813, occupied a cabin, and soon built houses for their families. Crisler's sawmill attracted other settlers to the area, and a still and a hemp mill soon located nearby. Crisler's operation continued until a flood changed the Whitewater River's channel. Another mill was built not long after on the new river channel.

The town of Alpine was laid out by 1832, reportedly named for the alpine-like rolling hills and the number of German settlers. The canal was built through Alpine by 1845, and a post office opened at Alpine on February 24, 1868. An 1885 report noted that the town contained a sawmill, a gristmill, and a railroad station. The railroad once had a spur track located here to the east.

In 1917, the town boasted a population of about 60. The size of the town is made clear by the many titles that E. I. Chance held. These included the position of postmaster, railroad agent, express agent, and owner of the local general store. While it still exists today, the town is no larger and the post office closed in 1966.

61.7 **CONNELL'S LOCK (#34)** – This was officially Lock #34. The remains of the composite lock, once consisting of stone lined with timber, are hidden in the woods to the west. The lock opened for service in June 1845 and was likely named for James Connell, one of the leaders of the Whitewater Valley Canal Company when it was chartered in 1842.

61.0 **BIDE-A-WEE** – This was the location of a mid-twentieth century summer camp. Ruins can be seen on the hillside next to the tracks. This area was a popular vacation and summer home location, with several other camps nearby. About a quarter of a mile south is the former site of a church camp, known as the Baptistery for its summer dunkings. To the west of the railroad is a rather "large" building known as the "Indiana White House" by locals.

60.4 **LIMPUS LOCK (#33)** – This was Canal #33. Little can be seen of the lock except a sign and lots of brush. James and John Limpus had built a gristmill near Alpine by the early 1840s, and several branches of the family lived throughout the area.

59.7 **COUNTY LINE** – This is the boundary between Fayette County, to the north, and Franklin County to the south. There are 92 counties within Indiana. **Fayette County** was created on January 29, 1818, from parts of Wayne and Franklin counties, as well as some unclaimed land to the north. The county was named for the Marquis de la Fayette, a French hero of the Revolutionary War. When the county was created, Connersville was a small village but it was designated as the county seat. It is still the only incorporated town, now a city, in the county. Fayette County still has a great deal of manufacturing in the Connersville area that is left over from its days as an early automotive manufacturing center. However, most of the county consists of small rural communities and farms. The population of the county is approximately 25,000.

Franklin County, named for Ben Franklin, was formed on February 1, 1811. During the first half of the 1800s, the county was the political center of Indiana. Governors James Brown Ray (1825-1831), Noah Noble (1831-1837), and David Wallace (1837-1840) were all from Brookville and served consecutive terms, giving them the name of "The Brookville Triumvirate." A fourth governor, Abram Hammond (1860-1861), was also from Brookville, the county seat of Franklin County. The county is very rural in nature in spite of being part of the Cincinnati Metropolitan Statistical Area. Its population is slightly less than 25,000.

59.6 GARRISON'S CREEK BRIDGE – This was Bridge #132 on the railroad. Garrison's Creek is believed to be named for Samuel Garrison, a settler in this area by the War of 1812. Garrison Creek is only several miles long, being formed when the South Fork and North Fork merge not far north of here. Both forks form near Glenwood about ten miles further to the northwest. Less than a mile southeast of here, Garrison Creek flows into the West Fork Whitewater River. This is where Colonel Shriver died during his survey to build a canal along the Whitewater River.

To cross the stream, the White Water Valley Canal Company built the Garrison Creek Aqueduct where the railroad bridge now stands.

59.5 GARRISON'S LOCK (#32) – Garrison's Lock, also known as Garrison's Creek Lock, was Lock #32. This rough-cut stone lock can barely be seen in the low brush beside the tracks. On September 13, 1836, a contract was issued to William Garrison for construction of this part of the canal.

For trains heading north, the grade in this area is the steepest on the railroad. It measures 1.1%, or just more than a one-foot rise for every one hundred feet of track.

59.4 PORTER'S CORNER – And now for something really different! This name comes from an early Whitewater Valley Railroad incident involving the tracks turning and a southbound steam locomotive not turning. Guess who the engineer was.

58.4 HETRICK'S LOCK (#31) – This was Lock #31. Jacob Hedrick was a taxpayer in 1811, the first year of the existence of Franklin County. He is often cited as one of the first settlers in the Brookville township. Some sources call the name of the lock Hedrick's Lock, and sometime during the 1800s the family name Hetrick became Hedrick.

Heading south, there is a large cemetery visible to the southwest. This is the Conwell Cemetery in Laurel. Markers at the cemetery state that it was founded in 1832. A number of Conwell family members are buried here.

58.1 NORTH LAUREL BRIDGE #131 – The railroad crosses a small stream as it approaches Laurel from the north.

57.7 LAUREL – The Laurel area was first settled in 1811 when the first major wave of settlers arrived. In 1816, the settlement of Somerset was laid out nearby. The Laurel area became the eastern end of the Whetzel Trace in 1818, when Jacob Whetzel, his son Cyrus, and a crew of axmen cut an east-west trail that began on the Whitewater River here, crossed the Big Blue River, and ended on the White River near Waverly, Indiana. The trace was a popular route for settlers moving across the state, helping to create a number of towns, including the new capital at Indianapolis.

In 1816, Edward Toner laid out the community of Somerset, which soon became a well-known trading center. During the early 1800s, there were numerous distilleries in the area, including the Webster distillery, which was operating by 1822. Things began to change when Reverend James Conwell of Laurel, Delaware (some sources say Laurel, Maryland), became Somerset's postmaster in 1831 and changed its name to Conwell Mills. He was elected to the House of Representatives in 1834. Conwell came to the area in an attempt to create a model town. With the existing alcohol industries, he looked to create a new town. One of the requirements was a town devoid of "spirituous liquors." The planned name of the town was New Baltimore after where Conwell had once lived, but it became Laurel after his other home. The post office opened in 1837. Later the two communities merged.

Because of the canal (which reached here in 1843) and later the railroad, Laurel soon became a warehouse town serving the surrounding countryside. Industries such as pork packing plants, copper shops, stone quarries, apple orchards and packing houses, and shipping companies soon located here. This again changed the characteristics of Laurel. A number of warehouses were built at Laurel to handle processed pork, wheat, lumber, and other products that could be shipped to market on the canal. An interesting example of this change was the Laurel general store, opened by Conwell in 1833. The building next became a pork packing establishment to serve canal boats, then changed back to a store. In 1874, John Colter opened a distillery in the large brick building, reportedly due to its location near the railway station.

In 1882, Laurel was still closely aligned with the former canal and railroad. A map from that year showed that there were several warehouses straddling the old canal. The railroad was primarily on the west bank of the canal, but a siding looped around the east side to serve several buildings. To the north of Commerce Street was a large stone cutting yard in an area once identified as the Laurel Canal Basin.

Immediately to the west of Laurel was the community of Somerset, with Mount Auburn to the northwest. Both of these were shown to be developments by F. A. Conwell.

While Laurel was never a major manufacturing center, there were a number of local industries. Among these in 1905 were the Brookville Canning Company; George W. Hunsinger's saw and grist mill; and Issac Weirs and Son, manufacturers of wagons and furniture. There were also a number of stone quarries in the area. For the railroad, there was a 30-car siding with the south switch just north of the passenger station and freight house. Stockpens and a grain elevator, located on the east side of the tracks, were once served by the railroad. Located just north of Pearl Street at Milepost 57.7, the passenger station once stood on the northwest corner of this crossing while the freighthouse stood across the tracks on the northeast corner. The passenger depot was abandoned first with all offices moved to the freighthouse. In 1951, the New York Central had an agency here that was open 8:00am-5:00pm daily except Saturday and Sunday. The office call code was "A".

Laurel was the birthplace of several interesting people. One was Francis A. Shoup, an Indianapolis lawyer who became a Confederate brigadier general. Shoup was born here in 1834, and graduated from the United States Military Academy in 1855. He served with the First United States Artillery and fought against the Seminoles in Florida. He resigned in 1860 to practice law, but soon moved south due to his "aristocratic inclinations and admiration for the South." He fought at battles such as Shiloh, Prairie Grove, Vicksburg, and Atlanta, and also held titles such as Inspector General in Arkansas and Chief of Staff for the commander of the Army of Tennessee. He wrote military textbooks, and was unique in calling for equal rights for African-Americans and their acceptance in the Confederate military. He later served as a professor at the University of Mississippi, and then the University of the South in Sewanee, Tennessee, where he is buried. Shoup is still known for his books about mathematics and metaphysics, and especially his essay *Uncle Tom's Cabin, Forty Years After*, which praised Harriet Beecher Stowe's anti-slavery novel.

Laurel is also the birthplace of Charles Murray. Murray appeared in 283 films between 1912 and 1938, and also regularly appeared on stage during that time. He primarily worked in silent film, including the 1925 *Wizard of Oz* and the 1927 *Life of Riley*. Many of his movies are now lost, but some have been preserved by the Library of Congress. The home that he grew up in is located at Washington and Baltimore streets. His star on the Hollywood Walk of Fame is at 1725 Vine Street.

A final unusual claim to fame for Laurel is that the last verified passenger pigeon in the wild was shot near Laurel on April 3, 1902. The passenger pigeon used to be the most common bird in North America, grouping in flocks of millions (or even billions). Their large numbers destroyed crops and pushed competitors, including large mammals, away from their feeding and nesting zones (an estimated 850 square miles in Wisconsin alone). As they were hunted, they were unable to defend themselves in smaller flocks and became food sources for both men and animals, until the last passenger pigeon died in captivity on September 1, 1914, in Cincinnati.

Today, Laurel has lost most of its glamour, with no large industries serving the canal or railroad. The population is approximately 500. Laurel is the home of the Laurel Hotel, the "premier steak and seafood restaurant in the Whitewater Valley," once Hunsinger's Tavern. This is an old-style hotel and restaurant that attracts people from across the region. Another historic feature of Laurel is the Old Jail, built in 1891 of local stone. It still stands along Commerce Street where the original Laurel Canal Basin once was.

WWV 25 passes an old home in downtown Laurel. Unfortunately, the house has since burned and only a few parts of the structure remain. Photo by Barton Jennings.

The Stone Industry

By the late 1800s, the stone/quarry industry became the leading industry in Laurel. Laurel has been the home of stone industries since the early 1800s. Many of the locks on the canal used stone from Laurel. The *First Annual Report of the Geological Survey of Indiana* (1869) reported heavily on the subject, stating that "blue Cincinnati limestone" is abundant everywhere around Laurel. This was recognized as a major source of building materials, especially sidewalks. It concluded that the "most valuable building-stone in the county, or probably in the State, is found in Laurel and Posey townships." The report specifically listed the D. H. Mook Limestone Quarry (two miles northwest of Laurel), the William Depperman Limestone Quarry (immediately west of the Mook quarry), and the Laurel Steam Stone Company (three miles west of Laurel).

Of particular interest is the Laurel Steam Stone Company. This company was organized in April 1900 to quarry some of the area limestone. The quarry had previously been the Derbyshire Falls Stone and Cement Company, which had entered receivership. Derbyshire Falls Stone had built a three-mile-long narrow gauge railroad about 1898 (based upon an article in the July 28, 1898, issue of *The Brookville Democrat*) between the quarry and the Cleveland, Cincinnati, Chicago & St. Louis Railway at Laurel to move their limestone. Reportedly, approximately fifteen cars of dressed stone were moved daily to Laurel for shipment to customers across the country. The company employed 100 to 150 people at the time, primarily cutting stones for sidewalk paving.

In the July 1903, Volume 26 Issue 3 of *Stone*, there was a short article about a possible expansion of the private railroad. The article stated: "The Laurel Steam Stone Company, which operates a quarry near Laurel, Ind., is planning to extend its private railroad from Laurel to Rushville, a distance of 18 miles. The company now operates the railroad from Laurel to its quarries three miles distant."

At the time, Laurel Steam Stone Company had an interesting mix of directors that later led to changes in the company. These directors included Caleb W. Pusey, Joel B. Pusey, Edgar O'Hair, John O'Hair, and Oscar Derbyshire. By 1903 the firm was in financial trouble, owing money to a number of parties, including some of the directors. Edgar O'Hair and the Puseys were owed money for the quarry equipment, rights of way, and railroad. This put John O'Hair and Oscar Derbyshire at odds with the rest of the board as they were essentially the ones that owed the money. The debt was finally settled when Edgar O'Hair, Caleb W. Pusey, and Joel B. Pusey gained control of the company in September 1904. The fortune of the company seemed to have turned around for a few years, but it shut down about 1915 due to the growing use of cement for sidewalks. However, even today, many communities and homes across the region still have sidewalks and walkways made from Laurel stone.

57.4 WEST FORK OF THE WHITEWATER RIVER BRIDGE – Known as Laurel Bridge, or Bridge #125, this bridge was rebuilt by the Cleveland, Cincinnati, Chicago & St. Louis Railway in 1906, using five deck plate girder spans. The bridge lasted until a flood in 1913 tore out two spans. To get the railroad back in service, the two spans were replaced by a timber trestle structure. Two new 66-foot deck plate girder spans were installed in 1914. The three older spans were replaced in 1925 to upgrade the entire structure. The bridge is reportedly 412 feet long and uses some of the piers and stone abutments from the original aqueduct of the canal.

This impressive deck-plate girder structure crosses the river which drains much of southeastern Indiana. This bridge has been a pain for the railroads ever since it was built. The river, which will now be visible off-and-on to the west, brings a large amount of drift downstream after most heavy rains. Details about the Whitewater River can be found on Page 9.

The Whitewater Valley Railroad operates a number of special events, including special freight trains for photographers. This train crosses the Laurel Bridge with a historic collection of freight cars. Photo by Barton Jennings.

Route Guide

The White Water Valley Canal also once crossed the river here, using a long aqueduct. The aqueduct was known as the White Bridge or the Laurel Aqueduct, and opened during September of 1838. Reports from the time stated that it was 392 feet long, cost $14,000 to build, and featured a towpath on the west side of the structure.

57.3 DAM ROAD – Dam Road follows the railroad from here almost to Metamora. To get to this road from Laurel, take Pearl Street east off of Highway 121 and turn right soon after crossing the Whitewater River.

57.2 LAUREL LOCK (#30) – Known as Lock #30, this is a double lock located in the woods to the west. Much of the stone for area locks came from the nearby quarries around Laurel. However, most of the cement or quicklime used came from Kentucky. One existing bill shows the order for 2000 barrels of quicklime at a cost of $2.62½ per barrel.

Not far south of Laurel Lock, the railroad comes alongside the West Fork Whitewater River again. Look to the west for some great views. The railroad again has a grade crossing with Dam Road.

56.5 JENKS' LOCK (#29) – A few walls of Lock #29 can be seen supporting the fill of the railroad to the east. In this area, the canal passed through the property of Samuel Jenks, according to the lawsuit *The Whitewater Valley Canal Company v. Henderson*. The suit was about who was harmed by the construction of the canal. The case provided documentation that Jenks, on June 15, 1835, "released to one Morgan, a commissioner of the state, the right of way for the canal through all the lands owned by him in Franklin county." It should be noted that some later documents, including many modern articles about the canal, use the spelling Jinks for this lock.

Off to the west in the West Fork Whitewater River is the Laurel (#4) Feeder Dam and Regulator. The canal between Brookville and the Laurel Feeder Dam was open by October 1843. This is the only remaining dam (of seven built) used to divert water into the Whitewater Canal. The dam was originally built of wood, but was washed out in the 1847 flood. (Flooding was a common problem. Major floods occurred in early 1847, late 1847, 1848, 1850 and 1852.) When rebuilt, concrete was used in its construction. From this point to Metamora, the canal is easy to see as it still holds water in this area. A great deal of dredging was conducted in early 2018 to widen and deepen the channel after years of sediment filling the remains of the old canal.

Just north of the feeder dam is Bridge #113. This short bridge crosses the feeder canal from the #4 Feeder Dam. This feeder canal is still used to water the canal from here through Metamora. Just south of the Jenks area is a 1.0% grade for northbound trains, created by the need to gain elevation over the lock and above the feeder dam.

The Laurel (#4) Feeder Dam to the west of the tracks is a popular local fishing attraction. Photo by Barton Jennings.

55.2 SIMONTON'S LOCK (#28) – Canal documents indicate that H. Simonton was issued a contract to build part of the canal on September 13, 1836. Lock #28 is clearly visible next to the tracks on the east side. It is a composite lock, with stone and timber construction. The lock has water passing through it, but is missing its gates and is not in use.

54.6 BRIDGE #111 – The tracks cross over the former canal here, using a two-span concrete box bridge.

54.5 DAM ROAD – On trains heading toward Metamora, this is the first crossing in what is called "triple crossing curve." The railroad crosses Dam Road three times in less than a quarter-mile. Just south of this crossing, the railroad bridges over the former canal on Bridge #109.

Just as the bridges were numbered by the New York Central, so were the curves. All started at the Cincinnati end of the route. It is an interesting coincidence that Bridge #109 is located in Curve #109.

WWV 25 passes through triple crossing curve near Leonards (Lennards). Photo by Barton Jennings.

54.2   FERRIS' LOCK (#27) – Back about Milepost 54.5, the railroad took off straight across the valley while the old canal stayed over against the hillside to the north. The lock, known as Lock #27, is barely visible across the pasture to the north. Lock #27 was built with cut stone and still stands, but without its wooden gates. Water from a small stream still passes through the lock.

Several families named Ferris lived in the Brookville-Metamora area during the early 1800s. Frederick Ferris moved here in 1811 from Vermont. Another Ferris, John W., was a farmer in the Brookville area. It is likely that the canal was named after some member of one of the Ferris families.

54.0   VALLEY VIEW – There are some fine views across several farms in this area, thus the name.

53.9   ICE POND – The pasture lands in this area between the railroad and the canal used to be used to produce ice in winter. The area would be flooded annually and the ice hauled to Cincinnati for storage and sale. In 1899, Sanborn indicated that the Cincinnati Ice Company had ice houses here, served by a rail spur.

According to several early Whitewater Valley Railroad sources, the curve south of this area is known as Curve #107, or Gard's Curve.

53.7   MURRAY'S LOCK (#26) – The canal and the railroad come back together near the former Lock #26. This stone and timber lock still exists and has water flowing through it, although it is missing its wooden gates.

The first mill in nearby Metamora was built in 1845 as a cotton mill by Jonathan Banes. The mill failed due to a lack of local cotton and competition with imported dry goods, available due to the water transportation. In 1856, the mill was changed to make flour, and the new owners were Murray and Banes. The next year, the mill

Route Guide

was acquired by John Murray and his John Murray & Son company.

53.4 **BRIDGE #108** – The railroad bridges over the canal.

53.3 **BRIDGE #106** – The railroad again bridges over the canal. In 1975, a Penn Central train derailed just south of here, ending freight service over the line between Boookville and Connersville.

52.7 **LEONARDS SIDING** – This siding was listed in the *Cleveland, Cincinnati, Chicago & St. Louis Railway Indiana Division Time Table No. 7*, dated January 1, 1936. It was not a stop for passenger trains in that year. According to the *State of Indiana Bureau of Statistics Eleventh Biennial Report for the Years 1905 and 1906*, the name should be Lennards, named for the H. R. Lennard Handle Company. An 1899 Sanborn map confirms this, showing the Lennard Handle Company as being one mile west of the Metamora post office. It was on a siding to the south of the mainline, with the former canal to the north of the mainline.

NYC 9339 leads a photo freight train by Leonards (Lennards) Siding. Photo by Barton Jennings.

Today, the siding is to the north and is used to switch trains during normal excursion operations. The west switch is at Milepost 52.9 while the east switch, known as Van Camp's, is at the grade crossing with U.S. Highway 52 at Milepost 52.6.

52.6 VAN CAMP'S – Van Camp's is at Leonards South Switch. Just east of Highway 52 is a former cannery later used as a stone finishing operation. According to several reports, this was an original cannery for the Van Camp's company. Other reports state that it was the Franklin Canning Company.

Downtown in Metamora on the southeast corner of Main and Bridge Streets was a drug store once owned by another Van Camp. In 1851, the drug store blew up from a gasoline explosion. This Mr. Van Camp and his mother perished in the explosion. Another Van Camp, Gilbert C. Van Camp, was born in nearby Brookville on December 25, 1814. At the age of 17, Gilbert began working at a local flour mill, and later learned tinsmithing, making tinware and stoves to sell. By the early 1860s, Van Camp had partnered with a fruit grower and a financier, building a cold storage warehouse in Indianapolis and later canning raspberries, blackberries, peaches and tomatoes in six-gallon cans. The demand allowed the company to expand, moving into a larger building by 1868. During this time, the firm began sending employees with wagon loads of cans and cooking pans directly to orchards, canning the fruit at the source. During the late 1870s, the name of the packing house was changed to G. C. Van Camp & Son.

In 1879 the company went bankrupt, and Gilbert Van Camp created the Van Camp Packing Company in 1882. To cut costs, the firm stuck with the most successful products: canned tomatoes, corn, and peas. Over the next few years, the plant burned and the Panic of 1893 sent the company into financial difficulties. Opportunity came along in 1894 when a local Indianapolis jobber brought a load of canned baked beans to the Van Camp plant to have them reprocessed. Gilbert's son Frank Van Camp tried some of the beans and found them to have no real taste. He added some Van Camps' ketchup to add flavor, and later began cooking beans and tomatoes together. This created *Van Camp's Pork and Beans with Tomato Sauce*. The product was an immediate success with national sales and a pack of house-to-house salesmen hitting local markets. By 1900, there were six plants across the country canning pork and beans, as well as evaporated milk. Each year, the company used more than six million cans and spent $1.5 million on advertising, dominating the market.

52.0 METAMORA LOCK (#25) – Metamora Lock, also known as Lock #25 of the White Water Valley Canal, is a beautiful example of a finished-stone canal lock, and is certainly one of the most photographed features of Metamora. While the lock doesn't work, it is solid but without its gates. Instead, the lock now holds a water wheel that is used to power the adjacent working grain mill, built here to take advantage of the water power from the canal. A relief bypass channel is to the north of the lock that is used to allow excess water to bypass the lock, protecting it from flooding.

The town of Metamora grew up around the lock and canal, and is now quite the tourist attraction. The town retains the character of a mid-19th century town. Many quaint period buildings now house shops. Located at the west end of Metamora, the restored mill is still in operation and is often the first stop for those who have arrived on the excursion train.

This marker explains Lock #25 and the water wheel that now occupies the space once used by canal barges. Photo by Sarah Jennings.

The mileposts of this line are measured from Cincinnati (CIN). Photo by Sarah Jennings.

Metamora Grist Mill

The Metamora Grist Mill has gone through a large number of changes over the years. The Metamora Cotton Factory was reportedly built in 1845 by Jonathan Banes as a three-story wooden cotton mill, equipped with 1000 spindles (the equivalent of 1000 spinning wheels). However, there was little local cotton production and competition from other mills made it unprofitable. In 1856, the mill was converted to a flour mill by Jonathan Banes and John Murray. The next year, John Murray acquired the mill and operated it as the John Murray & Son Mill. The mill was sold again in 1863 and became the Hoosier Mill owned by Thomas Tague. After the canal closed to navigation, the Brookville & Metamora Hydraulic Company was created to operate the canal for power. The mill was redesigned to use water from the canal after it was closed and used a breast water wheel (water feeds into the wheel at mid-level instead of at the top or bottom as other wheel types do) located in the middle of what was once Lock #25.

The mill was sold again in 1877, this time to William McClure, becoming Crescent Mills. The mill burned at least twice during the 1800s and was rebuilt after an 1899 fire. Frank Wright erected the new three-story brick flouring mill, reportedly with the capacity to produce fifty barrels of flour a day. In the early 1920s, the Brookville & Metamora Hydraulic Company found business unprofitable and cut off the canal's water supply. However, the canal through Lock #25 was kept open by the mill. A final change in the mill's design took place after a fire in the early 1930s. The new mill was only two stories and became the property of Ross Brumfiel who ground corn meal, and sold coal and mixed feed to area customers. Operations finally ended in 1941 when the feeder dam at Laurel was damaged by high water,

In 1947, the mill was acquired by the State of Indiana as part of the canal preservation effort. The Metamora Grist Mill, along with the Laurel Feeder Dam, Duck Creek

Aqueduct, and portions of the canal, were restored to operation by the State and are operated today as a State Historic Site by the Indiana Department of Natural Resources parks department. The mill is used as a demonstration project and houses both displays and a sales counter, in addition to the working mill.

The Metamora Grist Mill should be the first stop for any visit to the community. Photo by Sarah Jennings.

51.9 **METAMORA** – Metamora is the south end of the excursion train ride from Connersville. East of here, the railroad often operates short local trips, and demonstration canal boats are normally pulled on a short stretch of the canal.

Today, Metamora is a restored canal town, but the land was originally acquired from area Indian tribes on September 30, 1809, with the "12-Mile Purchase," the third treaty on the subject. On October 22, 1811, a 160-acre land grant was issued to Larkin Sims. A small community began to grow here and a post office was established nearby in April 1826. David Mount and William Holland platted out a formal community on the projected route of the canal in 1838, and on June 11, 1838, the post office was renamed Metamora (named for a Broadway play by J. A. Stone) from its original name of Duck Creek Crossing.

In 1853, the town was replatted and the town never outgrew this design and was never incorporated. When Metamora was originally designed, Main Street ran east to west and was more than 200 feet wide to allow the Whitewater Canal to be built down the center of the street. When the railroad replaced the canal in 1865, it too used the right-of-way through the center of Metamora. With the change, Metamora focused on milling (there were at least two mills here at one time), using the canal's water supply until 1936. These mills were used for processing cotton, grinding flour and making paper.

WWV 25 works its way through Metamora, alongside a dry Whitewater Canal. Photo by Barton Jennings.

A February 1899 Sanborn - Perris Map Company document clearly showed the railroad, former canal, and many of the industries in Metamora at the time. It showed that the railroad had a siding on the south side of the mainline, with the east switch just east of Columbia Street. Columbia Street is the only road that bridges the Whitewater Canal in Metamora. The passenger station once stood just to the west of the grade crossing with the building sitting on top of the old canal. It was torn down in 1946, and in 1951, the railroad listed no facilities here. However, there is still a passenger station in town. The former Brookville railroad station has been moved to Metamora. It is located on U.S. Highway 52 next to the Whitewater Valley Gateway Park. This wooden station was built in 1914 by the CCC&StL. Like the station in Metamora, the large station was built over the canal in Brookville, and since being moved to Metamora has been used as a restaurant and a meeting center. While in Brookville, the station was used for several years by the Whitewater Valley Railroad as their first base of operations.

The former Brookville, Indiana, depot stands almost forgotten alongside Highway 52 in Metamora. Photo by Barton Jennings.

The 1899 Sanborn - Perris map listed the A. J. Miller flour mill as being "not in operation." The map also stated that the population of Metamora was 400 and there was "No Fire Department & No Fire Alarm," and that the water facilities were not good. In fact, the map, which was used at the time for insurance risk analysis, was not kind at all about the firefighting ability of the town. Therefore, it is somewhat of a surprise that so many of the original buildings still stand at Metamora.

However, one reason that they do still stand is that in the 1930s, the main Brookville-Indianapolis road was moved north of town. This move preserved the town and prevented it from being destroyed by the road widening. Today, there are more than twenty buildings on the National Register of Historic Places here and Metamora is a center of antiques, flea markets and crafts. Most buildings are marked with their history. Metamora is still an unincorporated town and has a population of about 200. It is the home of Indiana's oldest and still operating water-powered gristmill, the Whitewater Canal State Historic Site, the Metamora Historic District, and canal boat rides using the *Ben Franklin III* pulled by horses. The annual Canal Days, held for more than forty years over the first weekend of October, is also a major part of the community. For visitors, the general rule is to look for a flag. If any flag is flying in front of a building, the store should be open.

The *Ben Franklin III* is used to provide rides on the canal during tourist season. Here it is docked in a dry canal while work is underway on the nearby Duck Creek Aqueduct. Photo by Barton Jennings.

Historic Structures

Canal towns like Metamora were located every few miles along the White Water Valley Canal. These towns were a source of fresh horses, food and lodging, and a place to buy and sell goods moved on the canal boats. Because of the trade, there was often a great deal of wealth in places like Metamora. Some of the buildings that still stand are the Odd Fellows Hall, the Martindale Hotel and Ezekial Tyner shipping office and storeroom, the Walker Brothers Warehouse, and many houses.

Any visit to Metamora should include a walk around town to admire the preserved buildings, many from the canal and early railroad era. A number of the buildings have a short history posted on them, and details of a few are presented here. Heading into town from the gristmill, a large brick house can be seen to the south. The two-story brick **Jonathan Banes House** was built about 1845 by Jonathan Banes and his wife Maria Mount Banes, the daughter of Metamora's founder David Mount. Banes was a noted construction contractor, having built part of the Whitewater Canal, and later the brick gristmill at Metamora. Artist Bernard Franklin LeParis later lived here.

Across the street to the east is the **Odd Fellows Lodge** (IOOF Building), at three stories high, the tallest building in town. The building was built in 1853 with the first floor used as a general store, for decades by the Gordon family. The post office was in the store for a while. The second floor was used as the town hall, and then later as a Knights of Pythias Lodge. The third floor was the Odd Fellows Lodge. The local Masonic Lodge was also formed in the building, created on May 23, 1857.

Route Guide

WWV 25 is posed in front of the IOOF Building in downdotwn Metamora. Photo by Barton Jennings.

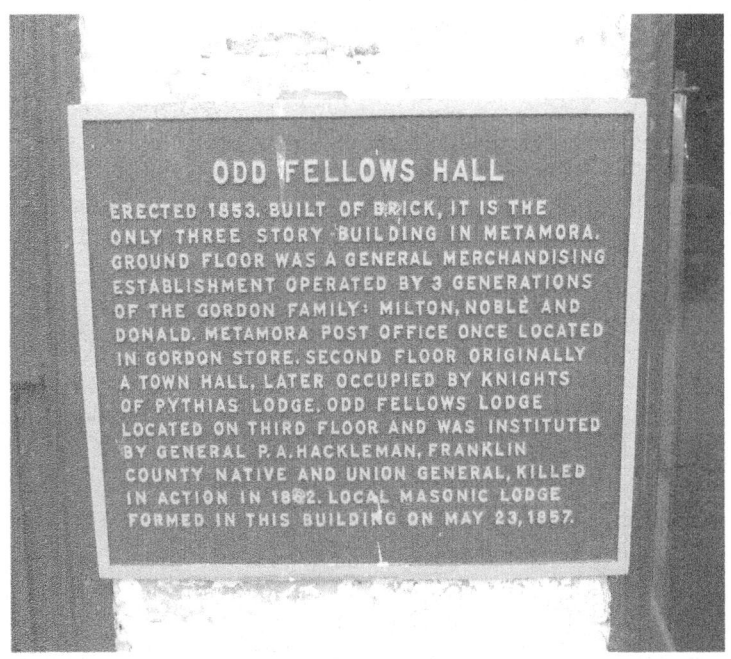

Many of the historic buildings in Metamora are identified by a series of plaques attached to their storefronts. This one provides the history of the Odd Fellows Hall. Photo by Barton Jennings.

At the corner of Main and Bridge Streets is the **Masonic Lodge** building. Local information says that the building was built in the 1840s, but the National Register says circa 1875. The building was reportedly owned over the years by a number of leading families, including Martindale, Watkins, Allison, and Wiley. The L. Allison & Son lettering comes from the name of the general store that operated here for many years. The Sons of Temperance used the second story for many years as the Temperance Hall Association. The Metamora Lodge #156 F&AM acquired title to the hall in 1888.

A block further to the east is the **Martindale Hotel**. Ezekial Tyner built the building in 1838 to house his storeroom and counting room. These were used as part of his duties acting as an agent for canal trade. His family was housed in the back. In 1856, Thomas Tague turned the property into a tavern. In 1870, Amos Martindale extended the building to the west and added lodging as the Martindale Hotel. A public dining room was also included.

On the north side of the canal is probably the most modern-looking building in downtown Metamora. This is the **Farmers Bank of Metamora**, a brick one-story building built in 1923. The bank was robbed twice in the early 1930s and eventually failed in the Depression and was liquidated in 1942. The original safe still stands inside.

On the north side of the canal at Bridge Street, known as Columbia Street in this area, is the former **Post Office** building. The building was built in 1854 for Gilbert C. Van Camp. Jesse and Ezekiel Washburn owned the building by 1861. By the 1880s, the second floor was the workshop of Joseph Staub and his "boots and shoes made to order" as well as saddles and harnesses. The post office used the first floor from 1920 until 1967.

At the east end of town on the north side of the canal is the **Metamora Christian Church**, a very photogenic building. This simple clapboard-clad, wood-frame church was built in 1871 and served as a church until 1970. The white church and its church-bell tower is often photographed as the canal boat passes by.

WWV 25 passes the Metamora Christian Church. Photo by Barton Jennings.

51.7 DUCK CREEK AQUEDUCT – The railroad crosses Duck Creek using Bridge #105. The bridge is a deck plate girder design. Soon after the railroad was opened, trains used a wooden through truss bridge to cross Duck Creek. Later, the CCC&StL replaced it with a steel girder bridge. The flood of 1913 took the bridge out and a new deck plate girder span was installed, the one that exists today.

According to the *Duck Creek Watershed Diagnostic Study*, prepared for the Franklin County Soil and Water Conservation District in 2008, Duck Creek forms at an elevation of approximately 1060 feet in the southeast corner of Fayette County. It then flows southwest through Metamora and into the West Fork of the Whitewater River just south of here at an elevation of 660 feet. The main part of the stream is about 11 miles long.

Just to the north of the railroad is the Duck Creek Aqueduct. An aqueduct is a bridge that carries a waterway, in this case the Whitewater Canal above Duck Creek. Duck Creek is lower than the canal, and controlling the water flow from Duck Creek would have been too much of a challenge to allow it to flow into the canal. Therefore, the aqueduct was built across the creek. The first aqueduct was a simple timber bridge built in 1843 that washed out during heavy flooding in 1846. The following year, a new aqueduct opened with a new design – a covered modified Burr arch truss. Today, this is the only remaining covered aqueduct in the country.

Bridge #105 stands next to the canal's Duck Creek Aquaduct. Photo by Barton Jennings.

Over the years, the bridge has been rebuilt, strengthened, and even raised to reduce the stress on the structure. The National Park Service reports that the aqueduct is "approximately 90' long, 25' wide, and 25' deep." The width of the canal is a bit more than 17 feet and the vertical clearance is 12 feet. The aqueduct is approximately 10 feet above Duck Creek, and it became the property of the Indiana Department of Conservation during the mid-1940s.

Also known as the Metamora Aqueduct and the Whitewater Canal Aqueduct, the structure was recorded by the Historic American Buildings Survey (HABS) in 1934. It is part of the Whitewater Canal Historic District, which was listed in the National Register of Historic Places in 1973. In 1992, it became part of the Metamora Historic District, also listed in the National Register of Historic Places, and named a National Historic Civil Engineering Landmark. It became part of the Historic American Engineering Record (HAER) in 2012, and became a National Historic Landmark in 2014. The aqueduct was also featured in an edition of *Ripley's Believe It Or Not*.

A feature of the aqueduct that confuses some is that it has several openings where some of the water pours out into Duck Creek. While some visitors think that the bridge is leaking, the openings are there to release excess water from the canal system.

WWV 25 passes the Duck Creek Aquaduct with a photo freight. Photo by Barton Jennings.

51.4 GORDON'S LOCK (#24) – This was also known as Millville Lock or Lock #24. This lock, since it was near a town, was built using cut-stone. The name of Gordon comes from the Gordon brothers who built a flouring mill in Metamora in the mid-1840s. A much larger mill was built at this lock in 1850. They then built a woolen mill next to their flour mill. Both burned and were rebuilt by Clifford & Davis. After the canal was closed, at least two mills operated here to use the water power of the canal. These two mills – a cotton mill and a flour mill, were joined by about seven houses as the town of Millville.

Today, the lock works again, having been restored in 1953 as part of the canal restoration in this area. It is used to keep water in the canal through Metamora, and for winter storage of the *Ben Franklin III*.

NYC 9339 passes by the restored Lock #24 for a photography event. Photo by Barton Jennings.

Heading south on the railroad, the former canal and then U.S. Highway 52 are immediately to the north (railroad-east). There are also a number of low hills in that direction that provide brilliant scenes during the spring bloom and fall color. Not far past the Millville Lock is a roadside park that includes a pavilion and information about the canal. The railroad and canal loop to the north and then back to the south, following an old bend in the river.

50.0 **END OF THE RAILROAD** – In 1974, a section of track between Metamora and Brookville washed out. Penn Central decided not to fix the damaged track and abandoned five miles of track from here to the north end of Brookville. Parts of this route have been replaced by the Whitewater Canal Trail. The rail route from Brookville to Valley Junction, Ohio, is still in service. The line is operated by the Indiana & Ohio Railroad, primarily to serve the Owens Corning plant at Brookville, and the new West Harrison flour mill of Siemer Milling Company.

WWV conductor, Nulltown. Photo by Barton Jennings.

About the Author

For almost three decades, Barton Jennings has been organizing charter passenger trains and writing the route descriptions, both for planning purposes and for the enjoyment of the passengers. These trips have been from coast to coast, often covering operations that haven't seen a passenger train in decades. In addition, he has written a number of articles about various railroads for rail hobby magazines. This book was created due to several of these charters that were conducted on the Whitewater Valley Railroad. Much of this information has been collected over many visits to the property, and thanks to the efforts of volunteers at the operation.

His basement has several rooms full of books, timetables and other documents about this and other railroads – important research items from a time long before today's internet. Today, Bart Jennings, after years working in the railroad industry, is a professor of supply chain management and teaches transportation operations. He also still teaches regulatory issues for the railroad industry, a way to stay in touch with the industry he loves.

Bart has operated several charter trains over the Whitewater Valley Railroad for photography purposes, and this guide started as information for the riders of those trips. Much of the book's information comes from internal railroad and canal records, government and public records, railroad workers, and conversations with old and new friends. It is hoped that you enjoy your adventure with the *Whitewater Valley Railroad: History Through the Miles*.

The author at Dearborn Tower, Connersville. Photo by Sarah Jennings.